You'll Go Blind

&

Other Lies They Told You About Loving Yourself

By: Jackie Weber

Imprint: Independently Published
Kindle Direct Publishing an Amazon
Company.   Seattle, Washington.
https://kdp.amazon.com/en_US/

Published in the US, Canada, UK, Germany,
India, France, Italy, Spain, Japan, Brazil,
Mexico, Australia (in English only).

Printed in the United States of America
ISBN: 9781973268246

First Paperback Edition

To all those who struggle to find the love
they owe themselves.

Coming soon from Jackie Weber

2020 *The Golden Rule is for Sissies & Other Lies They Told You About Loving Others*

2021 *Life Sucks, Then You Die & Other Lies They Told You About Loving Your Life*

Reader's Critical Acclaim for *You'll Go Blind & Other Lies They Told You About Loving Yourself*

"This book boils down all the essential parts of all the books that we don't have time to read. The chapters synthesize what it takes whole books to say. It is like the greatest hits album of self-love. It is perfect for the busy person looking for light and insight." – Robbyn, 50, married, mother of two and a dog, owner of the most positive attitude known to woman.

"The chapters were short and actionable with activities that are recursive. I loved hearing the humor in Jackie's voice. I felt relieved, hopeful, and calm while reading. Jackie makes all of this work feel necessary and do-able." – Jenn, 46, married, mother of two daughters, one dog, one hamster and one cat, and knitter of fantastic scarves.

"This book (don't tell my wife I read this kind of stuff!) is food for the soul. I was impressed with Jackie's research and am always a fan of the pop culture references sprinkled throughout (I, myself, love a good red stapler)." – Matt, 49, married, father of two daughters, inspiring screenplay writer.

"The more I read, the more I reflected about my own life situations aided by Jackie's personal anecdotes and activities. I found myself having major realizations about my own life paths, personal biases, and intentions. I also read a few chapters more than once – moderation and fear – and gained new insights the second read." – Bethany, Twenty-something, math teacher and expert of the long-distance relationship.

"I enjoyed the book more and more the more I read. I found myself not wanting to skip a word as I got into it. What makes this book work is how honest Jackie is with her readers. She leads by example with her own introspection and incredible willingness to truly bare her soul for all of us to see. That courage inspires courage in others." – Dan, 48, avid cyclist and scuba diver.

"I loved this very readable, useful book and I have already quoted the book." – Samara, powerful female principal, wearer of exceptionally sassy leggings.

"This book shows compassion for and an understanding of her readers' needs and feelings. Very insightful. An excellent pathway to increased happiness, love of oneself and control over one's life." – Connie, 75, retired, owner of *Mom's Fleece Company*.

"This book is about someone who accomplishes two journeys at the same time, journey from the author and your own personal journey. At the same time, I found I lost track of who I was reading about – Jackie or myself? Jackie is herself with her readers, both intelligent and vulnerable at the same time." - Guillermo, 53, passionate Latino with great hair.

"Well-thought-out and presented in a clear and concise manner that was also entertaining. A great read for that person willing to begin an insightful journey into self." – Joanne, 72, Adventurer and seeker.

"This book is like a good one-on-one conversation with a great friend. You share experiences, cry together and find ways to be the YOU you want to be. Jackie's insights and sincerity are evident and impactful." – Malory, 27, faithful wife, mother and friend, crazy enough to run every morning.

"Inviting, conversational and packed with action steps." – Julie, 55, newly retired grandmother.

Table of Contents

Acknowledgements

My sincerest gratitude goes out to my:

- Sister, Connie, who was the first person I talked to about this book. She didn't laugh at me once (in person) and helped me brainstorm, organize and problem-solve. Come to think of it, I don't think she ever doubted that I could do this – even when I did.

- Darling, Will, who even asked "When do I get to read it?" (twice!) when this is, definitely, not his kind of book. Will, has been so sweet and supportive, suggesting I should spend some time writing when we could have been out playing. He also never said out loud that I was wasting my time. He is my best friend, you "get me," he makes me laugh and consider maybe I do want to spend a year in an RV with him and Echo. I appreciate him. He has been patient while I learned to love myself separate from him.

- Best girlfriend friends, Kelli Imada, and Joanne Muntean, who have always talked through these issues with me, fully support my views on self-health and reflective practice, and voluntarily read these kinds of books.

- Dear friends, Robbyn Fernandez, Leonora Velasquez, and Rebecca Osburn, who graciously gave their time to read the first fifty pages and answer the question: "Do I bother to keep going?" Their feedback was invaluable.

- All of my first manuscript "beta" readers: Mallory Astin, Jenn Barr, Dr. Ron Cabrera, Joe Daw, Matt Dudek, Robbyn Fernandez, Dan Greenberg, Robyn Hamasaki, Connie & Dave Hooks, Bethany Konz, John McCluskey, Guillermo Medina, Joanne Muntean, Beth Stade, Janelle Stanton, Tracy Stegall, Julie Thorpe, Connie Weber, and Samara Williams.

- Colleagues at Boulder Valley School district who supported my reduced contract and my dream of writing this book. I could not have done it without the release of guilt these geniuses have allowed me: Cris Palmer, Dr. Ron Cabrera, David Woodward, Paige Wild, Bertha Orona, Dan Greenberg, Ann Hamilton, Jenn Barr, Dr. Samantha Messier, and Dr. Bruce Messinger.

Introduction

"Sooooo, tell me about your book," my colleague inquires, "is it about Math?" "Egads, no," I reply, "why would it be about math?" She, then points out that I have been a math educator for twenty years. Oh, *that math*. No, this book is not about math. This book is a funny exploration of what it feels like to love yourself and how to break down the lies that loving yourself is bad, wrong or selfish.

I see men and women, just like me, who are trying to figure out what really matters, what God has planned for them, how to make amends and thrive in the lives that they have been given. Yet over and over, all our lives, we are told that it is wrong to care for ourselves, want for ourselves, build a life for ourselves and love ourselves. This book is designed for all of us, who have fine lives, but feel that maybe something is missing, that there should be more to this life, that there are great things happening, but we just cannot see them. I understand those feelings and I want to share with you how I have sought and am still seeking, answers with the hope that my experiences will help you find the joy of loving, yourself.

Each of us is on our own private journey, but that doesn't mean that we are alone in this life. We are guided by God, supported by family and cheered on by all of our friends. My journey has been a successful one in many aspects, and a catastrophic train wreck in others. I have had super-star years and let's-just-forget-that-happened years. We all have. The beauty of this life is that we are meant to have both – dark and light, good and bad, yippee and good grief. And through all of those we have love.

Love has the potential to be a cliché, so let me clarify. When I use love in this book, I mean the love we have for ourselves, our neighbors, our spouses, our children, our dogs and a fresh loaf of warm and crusty French bread. Love is romantic, but it is also practical and divine, and earthly. First Corinthians, Chapter thirteen versus four through seven, tell us that "⁴ Love is patient, love is kind, it isn't jealous, it doesn't brag, it isn't arrogant, ⁵ it isn't rude, it doesn't seek its own advantage, it isn't irritable, it doesn't keep a record of complaints, ⁶ it isn't happy with injustice, but it is happy with the truth. ⁷ Love puts up with all things, trusts in all things, hopes for all things, endures all things." In laymen's terms, love sucks it up and deals with it. Love is grateful for the fight because of the grace that follows. Love will share the crusty bread with a stranger. Love is what dogs do. Love is what humans hope to do. Love is what we need to do for and ourselves each other. If you have never considered that particular scripture through the lens of loving yourself then give it a try. We should be patient and kind with ourselves. We shouldn't be jealous of others, rude to ourselves, keep a record of complaints for ourselves or allow ourselves to be treated with injustice.

It has taken me forty-some years to begin to understand the depth and power of love. I am merely scratching the surface, but somewhere in the last two years I felt prompted to share what I am learning with you. To share my journey with you. This book, which I hope holds many ah-ha moments for you, has been inspired by experience, an obscene number of women's magazines, an expensive array of self-help books, many lengthy and satisfying conversations with myself, and lots of prayers. I am not a PhD., licensed psychologist or clerical advisor. I am just a woman who is blessed with the gift of lessons learned and a knack for encouraging others be their best selves. It is my hope that this book feels like a great conversation with a good friend; one that opens your heart and mind, smacks you with reality and then wraps you gently in a nice fleece blanket and hands you a cup of cocoa, or a nice shot of whiskey, whatever your preference may be.

You'll Go Blind & Other Lies They Told You About Loving Yourself is written to shed a humorous, reflective and engaging light on our lives. The activities will guide you, but the learnings will be your own, personal, lessons. When you come to an activity you may choose to read it, fully engage in it, or skip it all together. They are there to help you reflect on your personal situation, but this is not a book with homework assignments and excessive demands. This book is a combination of reflections, stories, research, commentaries and insights that have moved through the Wonka Chocolate Factory of my mind from a variety of very normal and not terribly extraordinary sources. An early reader asked me what gives me the right to write this. Nothing, really. I do not yearn to tell you how to live your life. I do hope that we share similar experiences and worries, successes and joys. The pages that await you, dear reader, are my reflections, prompted by what I see every day, and grounded in real life. We will travel this journey together.

Sometimes we need to guide each other as we learn from the events in our lives - how we live, how we love, how we survive the challenges in our life, and how we embrace every day – even the days when we cannot possibly see a silver lining. Some of my deeper thoughts come from just paying attention to the world; some come from painful and life-altering events and circumstances. Some come from chick flicks, some from songs. Some come as answered prayers; all come exactly as I need them. We will also gather wisdom from the likes of Mr. Spock, Mother Teresa, P!nk, Jen Hatmaker, and Paulo Coelho. And may Dwayne "The Rock" Johnson protect your inner child from negativity as he does mine.

Please know that I wrote this as if I was sitting across the table from you over breakfast at a little local restaurant. I see you, we share a box of tissue, blow milk out of our noses from laughing and occasionally reach out for the other's hand. It is written informally, as a conversation might be. It is written with my voice as well as my heart. Each little Demi-Chapter is titled after a theme representing a common social lie. The Demi-Chapters are designed this way to make the reading easy to pick up and easy to put down when the day-to-day must continue. For me, the ease of reading one short topic allows me time to process and the thoughts to marinate in my head so that when I need to reflect on them, they are tender, juicy and ready to be chewed upon.

Don't be aggressive with this book. Our lives are busy enough, we should not rush ourselves when we read for pleasure or healing. Take time to read a little and savor it. Read it when you need it. Read it when you are sitting in a quiet place or just looking for a quiet moment on a busy commuter train. Read it with friends. Read it in the bathtub, with or without friends. Read it perched on a ledge looking over a beautiful canyon because that is where the idea for it was born. Read it one Demi Chapter at a time or devour the whole thing in one sitting. Don't rush. Don't ever, ever think "I need to finish this book, so I can…" This book is not designed to be a "must do" – it is for you to read, to reflect, to learn, to love, to feel a sense of joy and to remember a sense of yourself.

As you read each section, you may find that some of the ideas strike you now, some you may wish you had read a decade ago, some you won't need for another decade. As we live a reflective life, we collect the nuggets that we need to hear, when we need to hear them. We should embrace whatever it takes to remind us to live the best life we can. For some it is prayer. For others, meditation. My father finds regular animated conversations with the dog quite stimulating. These are the sources in our lives that prompt us to think deeper, feel deeper, and smile a little more. I have changed and grown dramatically in my ability to love myself, love others and love my life. All my life, even before writing this book, I was collecting articles, quotations, and photos of those clever signs sold in Amish décor shops (Who knew they so inspiring?). The wrappers from the Dove Promises Dark Chocolate candies gave me the final push to make this happen. To my surprise, every day since then, I have found something I wanted to share with you, my friends. In a way, the reflections I included here my progress through the challenges of loving myself. I hope that my journey in some way helps you – even if it is only to let you think, "Wow, I am so glad I am not her." It was my pleasure to write this for you and my hope that you will laugh a little, reflect a little, and begin to recognize that you can love yourself without going blind.

"If you celebrate your differentness, the world will, too. It believes exactly what you tell it—through the words you use to describe yourself, the actions you take to care for yourself, and the choices you make to express yourself. Tell the world that you are a one-of-a-kind creation who came here to experience wonder and spread joy. Expect to be accommodated. (11)"

— Victoria Moran,
Lit From Within: Tending Your Soul For Lifelong Beauty

Demi-Chapter I: Lovely

Let me tell you a story
Of a little boy who had lost his way
In search for something to make it a better
day…

Does anyone love me?
Does anyone care?
Is anyone out there
That finds me lovely?

Don't you know I love you?
Don't you know I care?
And I will always be here
And I find you lovely

Shawn McDonald, "Lovely"

You make everything lovely. Isn't this the most wonderful sentiment? Who does not feel all warm and squishy inside thinking that they, all by themselves, make things lovely? And not just things. *Everything.* I make *everything* lovely. _You_ make _everything_ lovely. Just by being there. Just by being you. Now, you must see why the book starts with this one. This is a write on the mirror in lipstick kind of statement. For those who don't use lipstick, maybe it's a write on your pancake with maple syrup kind of statement. It is so sweet. And wonderfully kind to whoever reads it.

We make even the mundane lovely. For example, I make mowing the lawn lovely. I do. I just finished mowing the 15' by 20' patch of green that I call my lawn. And it is lovely. I was lovely doing it. My arm muscles taut with exertion, my hair blowing super-model-esque in the evening breeze. Even the dirt smudge on the side of my face... why, that just highlights my cheekbones: Lovely! I did not always think I made things lovely. As a teen, I often struggled with what was my whole purpose in life. I tried to conform. If I saw someone doing something that seemed lovely, I would try to copy it. It was only when I started my first teaching job in a small rural school in

Ohio that I started to see my own lovely. My ability to make mathematics fun, engaging, and a place of success for students was my first awareness that we can

make small bits of another's life lovely. Once I realized the truth in this, I began to be able to accept that there were other areas that I could spread my lovely as well.

Try this first activity. It will ease you into the activities in the book.

Activity 1.1.1 Lovely-making

Use this sentence frame: I make

_____ lovely. Fill in some fun items. Soon you, too, will believe that you make everything lovely. And you DO! That is the pure beauty of this tiny affirmation.

One day in June 2012, I made my friend's birthday lovely, even from 1300 miles away. I not only remembered her birthday (because we specifically sat at breakfast one day and entered them into our electronic calendars together), but I bought a lovely book and a card that made me laugh out loud in the greeting card aisle. Do you laugh out loud in the greeting card aisle? You really should try it – it is great fun and terribly embarrassing for those in the aisle with you. I put the card and book in the mail on exactly the right day. She received it on her birthday and know that she was loved. So, not only do I make birthdays lovely, I also make miracles lovely, since it was a miracle that the hitherto described gift was even purchased.

I make text messages lovely because I have finally upgraded to a cranky but high-tech phone that comes with its own Emojis (☐). I make yoga pants and horribly colored t-shirts lovely because I wear them to the dog rescue to walk lonely and eager-to-please doggies. Ok, that one might be a stretch – the yoga pants thing – but darn it, I'm going for it. Each day there are countless things that I do to make this world lovely. And you do too. Activity 1.1.2 will help you find your lovely.

Activity 1.1.2 What Did You Make Lovely Today?

What did you make lovely today? You may need to think about this because it is not our natural American instinct to think well of ourselves. It is the first Demi Chapter of a book of reflections, so we are just warming up. Start from the beginning of the day. As you are thinking through your day you may get tired of smiling and just accept the fact that you do make everything lovely.

You make every day lovely when you smile at a friend and even lovelier when you smile at a stranger. Not in that creepy, "How you doin'?" kind of way but in the, "Hi. I sincerely hope you are having a nice day," kind of way. You make your child's or spouse's or partner's or pet's day lovely when you hug them, pick up their dirty socks without a snarky comment, whip up a lovely breakfast burrito to send them on their way or give them a good scratch on the butt – even husbands like this.

So, skeptics, I hear you. Sometimes we make mistakes. Sometimes we say things or write things that turn something ugly. Yes, granted, we do. But think of it this way. That one tiny thing is inside a bigger thing that we can make lovely. Perhaps I made a sarcastic comment in response to a colleague's heartfelt suggestion in a meeting. Ok, I didn't make that moment lovely, but I hopefully made that person's day lovely once again by sincerely apologizing and making my own suggestion that humbly opened myself up for bashing.

We are not perfect creatures (see Demi-Chapter III) but our goal really should be to make everything lovely and to return to loveliness anything we besmirch with our humanness. Ultimately, when we believe in

ourselves and our own personal loveliness
then we make life lovely and life is
everything.

Demi-Chapter II: Be you

---

*If you are always trying to be normal,
you will never know how amazing you
can be.*

Maya Angelou

Be free. Be happy. Be you. Are you happy with who you are? How you are? How you look, how you feel, what you do for a living? No one is entirely happy every moment of every day, but if you are not mostly happy with your life, you have a few choices, all of which start with accepting who you are right now. Once you have accepted who you are, you can decide if there are aspects of your life and your behavior that you can change. Notice I did not say that you will change who you are – you cannot do that – you are who you are, and you will learn to love and care for who you are. You can and may need to change your behaviors and certain external parts of your life. Happiness, however, is entirely an inside job.

It is ok if you change your behaviors, your opinions, or your beliefs throughout your life. That is expected. The trick is to be happy with you right now. My favorite yoga instructor is Sarah Ivanhoe. She doesn't know that she is the only one who has ever moved me to the point where I almost have a yoga "practice." One of the reasons is her complete awareness of the reality of her audience. In her *Candlelight Yoga* series, she encourages her students to engage in a stretch and to go to "Your all the way, for right now." I love that because it suggests that we both accept where we are, love and appreciate how far we can go, and look forward to what we might be able to do in the future. She also refers to yoga breaths as a "hollow Darth Vader sound." She's a Yoda yogi! What's not to love?

There is a certain freedom to accepting our own true selves, even if only one small step at a time. The Blue-footed Booby (pictured on the next page), besides having a most entertaining name, is a proud and colorful creature who, I think, wouldn't change his foot color for the world. He accepts who he is and uses his flashy blue feet to attract mates. Whereas, I, only quite accidentally, just learned to accept my hair color – the thing I often used to attract mates.

All of my life, I have had this rather interesting blond hair that pops out of my head a "dishwater blond" color, almost brown, and then within days, starts to lighten due to sunshine, chemicals in the city water, or nothing at all. It just lightens. This leaves me, quite irrationally, with perma-root. Not only that, but once it grows out it takes on the color of rust and has this orange tint. I wanted desperately to be a real Legolas Elvin blond, with ash highlights and none of what I saw as weird rusty dishwater color. This was the prevailing feeling for, oh, about 30 years.

I colored the roots and the red out of it. Constantly. Then, about January of my 40th year, about eight months before the official 4-0, I just stopped. I was tired and annoyed with the constant effort and the underwhelming satisfaction that came with the monthly chore. I just did not want to bother with coloring it any more. I wasn't embracing the gray – that's still a challenge for me – but I embraced that my roots were dark and had gold highlights in them. I actually dyed my hair back to my natural color (which, ironically, is also what Clairol calls natural blond) to rid myself of the ash blond ends. Then I just let it grow out and be what it was. About three weeks after this conscious decision, Will stopped me one day and quite innocently commented, "your hair matches your eyebrows." He did not say "your hair actually matches your eyebrows for once," but, basically, he could have. My first response was, of course, "Dude, WTF?!" but I did not say that because I knew he was right. It was finally natural. It was finally my hair. Now I love it. I can finally appreciate the depth and variation of the highlights I never noticed before. Ok, I have to admit that occasionally when looking in the mirror and spotting the gray hair I burst into a rendition of Burl Ives' "Silver and Gold," but I do love the gold now. And now I see that the red and gold *actually are* also in my eyebrows (luckily the gray is not yet). I see the sun shine on it through the sun roof and I wonder why I kept it hidden for so many years. Maybe it would be a small accomplishment for others, but for me, who has always been so hair-proud, it is nothing short of liberating. At forty I have the best hair I have ever had and most importantly, I like it. I've given myself the moniker of gold-haired booby. Wanna see me dance?

Activity 1.2.1 I Love Me. I Love Me Not.

Circle the number between 0 and the 10 to indicate your acceptance, satisfaction, and appreciation of each area of your life. Be honest. How you judge yourself on each of these areas of your life will tell you where to start. 0 represents Complete Rejection of myself and 10 represents Total Acceptance of myself:

My body (shape, size, physique)

0 1 2 3 4 5 6 7 8 9 10

My appearance (specific attributes)

0 1 2 3 4 5 6 7 8 9 10

My intelligence

0 1 2 3 4 5 6 7 8 9 10

My career success

0 1 2 3 4 5 6 7 8 9 10

Myself as a spouse/partner

0 1 2 3 4 5 6 7 8 9 10

My parenting

0 1 2 3 4 5 6 7 8 9 10

My relationships with others

0 1 2 3 4 5 6 7 8 9 10

My ability to keep it all together

0 1 2 3 4 5 6 7 8 9 10

My housekeeping

0 1 2 3 4 5 6 7 8 9 10

Other important area

0 1 2 3 4 5 6 7 8 9 10

If your score falls lower than a five on any of the charts, then your first step is to address your acceptance of yourself in those areas. When you reject yourself in any area of your life, it impacts every area of your life, your confidence, how you interact with others, and situations all through your life. Feeling bad about who you are will eventually taint the very situation you are trying to preserve.

What gets in the way of our loving

ourselves and just being who we are? Our boundary issues: our need to people-please and be accepted by others. Can I get a Hallelujah? I'm over 40 now and still struggling with this – especially at work. Intellectually, I know that I am good at my work (and lots of other things), but if there is conflict at work, I immediately start to find fault in myself and unhappiness because I am not beloved by my colleagues. When we define our worth by the approval of others, we lose our own perspective on everything that we are. Having an idea about who you wish you were or who you think you should be obscures your understanding of who you actually are and what you should be doing with your life. It is exhausting denying who you are or who you have become. Do you find yourself not speaking, dancing, helping, laughing, or doing what in your heart you need to be doing just because you "shouldn't" or "can't"? If so, then you must be exhausted. I know I am. Just writing these words I can feel that I am not fully aware of myself. I am in discovery mode, after all of these years. I am excited to get to know me again, but I am scared of what I am going to find out about myself. Just today a thought flitted across my mind that after all these years in public education, maybe I have accomplished all that I need to do and now it is time for the next calling. That's pretty exciting and pretty scary, but if I accept who I am and allow myself to be just that, then I will be ready when the time comes. I can already feel the pull and it is exhausting to pretend it isn't there. The only way to survive a rip-current is to swim parallel to shore and let the current deposit you somewhere further down the beach.

Just acknowledge the pull and swim with it.

There comes a time, a person, or a situation that helps the message sink in. Octavia Spencer, actress who has played a wide range of roles, including winning an Academy Award as Minnie Jackson in *The*

Help, said that even though her mother told her all the time to stay true to herself, it wasn't until she worked with Whoopi Goldberg and Whoopi said it, that it finally stuck (2015). Ellen DeGeneres (2009) speaks about her coming out as the moment that everything was stripped away, and she had to love who she was because everyone was watching her. If any of you remember that time, Ellen absolutely blossomed. Her energy was no longer absorbed by hiding. She knew that not everyone would accept her, but not everyone needs to. She is complete in who she is, and she did it with bravery and such good humor that I couldn't help but admire her courage.

The fear of being different, being judged, being seen as less by others limits our ability to embrace who we are and all we have to offer. Alexander Robbins, author of *The Power of Quirk,* advises us to embrace our quirkiness so that we can be our real selves, our truest selves, our we-est selves, your you-est self, my me-est self. While a rather Suessian sentiment, it is telling us to put ourselves out there for everyone to see. When you don't share it, when you keep it hidden away, the whole world loses. I know that once I regained my song and once again took up dancing in the kitchen (and Home Depot aisle, and checkout lanes…) a huge weight was lifted. I had pretended too long.

Dr. Sarah Lewis is author of *The Rise: Creativity, the Gift of Failure, and the Search for Mastery*, served on President Obama's Arts Policy Committee and is currently the Du Bois Fellow at Harvard University. She has held positions at Yale's School of Art, the Tate Modern, and the Museum of Modern Art in New York, and her essays have been published in Art forum and The Smithsonian. At a keynote speech at a conference for educator leaders I attended in 2015 she asked us to realize that when we limit the ideas we share because of what we think others might say, we may be giving up our own, possibly correct. When we do this as a response to the incorrect thinking of the majority around us, our fear of standing out, of being right, of being ourselves, we miss an opportunity to move the situation or solution forward and often we don't even realize it.

Because we stay silent, the whole world loses. The movie, "The Holiday" is one of my seasonal favorites because it is schmaltzy and affirming and just good fun. The best line in the movie is when Iris realizes, "You should be the leading lady of your own life." Or leading man. Are you playing an extra because you don't see yourself as a star?

After 40, 25, 15, 75 years, is it possible to shake off the labels we have taken upon ourselves (whether rightfully or not)? I think you will find that the answer is yes. Quite certainly yes. Mostly. It is possible, but it is not easy unless you are willing to be really honest. You may find that you aren't quite there yet with yourself or all of the labels that have been assigned to you. Todd Henry, at that same 2015 conference of educational leaders, challenged us to ask ourselves "What am I doing right now that doesn't seem like me? Am I trying to be someone else?" I took it as a personal challenge to find my own answer. The point is a sharp one. Are you being genuinely you?

Activity 1.2.2 Who Are You?

Consider the circles of this diagram. answer with the first thing that comes to your mind.

Who am I?

1. What am I good at?
2. What do I like best about myself?
3. What do I love doing?
4. Does the outward face I give the world match the inside me?
5. What is unique about me?

6. What do I value?

You may have to tackle one thing at a time. I suggest you start with the most uncomfortable part of your life. Is there any area of your life that feels like a too-small wool sweater on bare skin? I will pick one as an example. I have a terrible fear of being incompetent – in anything – and that someone will notice. My 1-10 chart is at, like, 1.87 or something. If I feel incompetent, it is game over. Now, sometimes I label myself incompetent because I make a mistake. Sometimes I imagine that someone else labels me incompetent. I have never actually been told I am incompetent by anyone. Ever. Yet the chance that it might happen haunts me like a Marley to my Scrooge. This used to send me in spasms of incapacitation and ulceration. But now one simple question pops me out of it. Is the label true? And, in general, I can get a grip on myself and admit that, no, in fact, it is not true. This works for not-yet-assigned labels as well. Let's say that you feel your true self has lime green dreadlocks, but you fear that the other lawyers in your firm and potential clients might label you a weirdo-alien-hippie. There is a paradigm that is,

> Accept and acknowledge your own brilliance. Stop waiting for others to tell you how great you are! Believe it for yourself. – Iyanla Vanzant

thankfully, shifting from old perceptions of professionalism, much to the dismay of my suit collection, but the fear of not being taken seriously is still a valid one. So, ask yourself: am I a weirdo-alien hippie? If you are, then celebrate that they finally labeled you correctly! If you are not, then you are not, and no label, opinion or bottle of hair color will make you one. Color your hair, embrace who you are. Your confidence and competence as an attorney will still be very apparent now that the real you has arrived on the scene. You may have to ease into it, but your colleagues and clients know, trust and love you. If they don't then maybe the bigger question is where can you go where they do? Let the dreads fall where they may.

Activity 1.2.3 Daily Affirmations

We are not talking about easy work, so here are some daily affirmations to try on for size. If you like one or two of them, keep them at the ready when you doubt yourself or your strength to let the real you shine through.

The essence of being human is that one does not seek perfection. – George Orwell

I offer no resistance to myself as I currently am. I accept myself in this moment the way I accept a tree or cloud. I simply exist. There is no need to change anything right now. I accept myself as I am. I accept myself. I accept myself. – Martha Beck

No need to hurry. No need to sparkle. No need to be anyone but oneself. – Virginia Wolff

Demi-Chapter III:
Healthy

"Being well is the decision. *Living* well is
the bonus."

Oprah Winfrey

Take good care of yourself. I am half
inclined to say this one is obvious. But it is
not obvious. It is painfully, sometimes
fatally, not obvious. When I lived in my cute
little 900 square-foot bungalow built for a
family of 1.75, I kept this phrase,
conveniently printed on the inside of a Dove
candy wrapper, lying (not even posted, but
just lying) right out in the middle of
everything on top of my toaster oven, which
took up about a third of the counter space in
my tiny kitchen. I still have it, in the same
place in a newer, slightly larger kitchen.
This note makes me chase it around when the

wind blows, but then I am always looking at it. And it makes me smile when I see it. Usually, it inspires an "Oh, yeah, I should do that!" with a smiley face and a little dance, rather than the "Oh, damn, I messed up again" with a frowny face and another Oreo. Other than taping it to a board that smacks me on the head every time I open the cheese drawer in my refrigerator, I could not think of a better place to put it. And it works.

So, why *is* taking care of our health such a crucial element of loving ourselves? Because without this one, the rest of the book is irrelevant. Take good care of yourself does not only mean eat right, exercise, and take vitamins. It also means doing all the other things in all of the other Demi-Chapters that make up this book. Plus, some. It means doing what needs to be done for you to live a long and happy life.

Yet, as important as we all recognize this is, most of us do not do it as we should. There is an entire multi-gazillion dollar industry designed to respond to the fact that most of us don't do it as we should. Sometimes we don't do it out of a perceived lack of time. Sometimes we don't do it out of a perceived lack of energy. Sometimes we don't do it because we don't feel we are worth the effort, or it will hurt too much, or we'll get behind at work, or our loved ones will feel ignored, or we will feel guilty, or etc., etc., etc. I am still working on this one myself, so I know all of the excuses and use them regularly myself.

The true mind twist on this one is that the less we take care of ourselves, the less likely we are to be there to take care of others. In a Kaiser Permanente member newsletter segment entitled "The Joys of Letting Go" the author reminds us, "If you're not feeling your best, you won't have as much to offer your loved ones." Logically, we know this, but so few of us do it. This is a wildly difficult lesson for women who tend to care for others at the expense of themselves. Men are not immune, however, and often work long and hard hours to provide for their families at the expense of their own health.

It takes tremendous chutzpah to step up and say to yourself, your partner, your friends, your kids, your boss – I need to do things differently for my own health. Our society sees this as weakness. It's not "The American Way," as Cadillac would like us to believe. But this is not weakness. This is strength. At a point in my life I had a 41mile commute, which took at least an hour, often longer, to drive one way. My back, my hips, my neck, my nerves, my family and my love of driving, all took a toll. I was not able to move closer to work and, with the economy in a tough place, changing jobs was an unlikely solution. After several health and relationship struggles, I finally had to admit that I was not taking care of myself. I worked with my supervisor at the time, a kind and sympathetic woman, to allow me to work from home one day a week and to drive, when possible, at off peak times. Just this small tweak in my schedule rebooted my ability to care for myself and I felt all areas of my life respond accordingly. This, obviously, is not a solution for everyone, but merely an example of how I needed to put on my big girl panties and take care of myself. That lasted a year and made a great difference, but once the supervisor retired and the policy changed, I was forced to reevaluate everything work-related. I am still doing this. But I know I must make changes in order to care for myself. Years later, I did move closer to work, and now I see that there is more to address. Keep reading to see how the saga unfolds!

Putting the knowledge into action is the hard part for all of us. I don't think any of you would argue that being healthy isn't, well, good for you, but it can be overwhelming to know how to find the time, money, energy and support for what you need to do. Try Activity 1.2.1. Set a two-week timeline and, if you need to, start a journal or download an app to hold yourself accountable. Tell a friend and use him or her as your daily report. Call it support and report. If you use social networks, advertise your new pledge to care for yourself and report out every evening. Ask your friends to support you. Ask those you know who are successful in this category to share their strategies with you. Explain to your family why you want to feel better (and how it will benefit them) and ask them to support you with specific things that they can do to help you stay focused and positive. Take notice of how you feel, what is different or better, and report these as well. Once your loved ones and colleagues see the difference in you, they will understand and support your need to be healthy. You may face resistance that causes you to doubt yourself or weaken your resolve. Stay strong knowing you aren't doing this on a whim and it is the right step for you. If you can stay strong you might even encourage them to take healthy steps as well. After a few months, you may decide to repeat this process and select another area of your life to focus on. That is up to you, but never give up on taking care of yourself.

Activity 1.3.1 A brainstorm of health!

Let's brainstorm. Think about the areas of your life where you are not taking care of yourself. Is it nutrition? Exercise? Stress relief? Emotional torture? Not enough sleep? I ask you to focus on one, just one, for a few minutes. Ask yourself these questions and jot down everything you think of:

- *What is in the way of your taking care of yourself in this area?*

- *Are there small things you can do to improve your care for yourself?*

- *To whom do you need to talk about your need to take care of yourself?*

You are not asking for permission but working through your needs with the people in your life who are impacted.

O *When will you start? Set a specific date. No excuses and postponements!*

If you have finished the activity feeling you have too many areas and you just don't know where you should start with being healthier, then start with your eyes closed. Sleep. Beautiful, healing, sleep. Gretchen Rubin, author of *The Happiness Project,* started her year-long pursuit of happiness with an earlier bedtime. According to a 2012 American Heart Association report, a lack of sleep causes in increase in stroke risk. Insomniacs are twice more likely to suffer a stroke than those who regularly get sufficient sleep. There is also research that shows that sleep deprivation decreases memory recall, both short and long term, weakens the immune system and slows the metabolism, causing weight gain. It also makes us crabby and no one wants that.

Are you not getting sleep because you keep your phone next to your bed? Try taking a break. Doree Shafrir, the executive editor of BuzzFeed, takes a break from her phone twice a day and then leaves it in the kitchen when she goes to bed at night to allow herself to truly disconnect. Start a routine near bedtime every night – low lights, turn off the electronics, put down the can't-put-this-down novel (this is my sleeper's Achilles' heel), stretch, pray, snuggle with a loved one and, as often as possible, sleep until you wake up naturally.

If you get plenty of sleep, try getting up from your chair more often during the day. Those who sit for six or more hours a day have a 37% higher mortality rate (meaning they die earlier, in this case), then those who sit for less than three hours a day. Stand at your desk, take 5-minute walk breaks every hour. Wiggle! Just move. My office mate, Sam, instituted one-minute dance-offs. I prefer cheesy 80s music to which I shake my groove thang. "Beat it," anyone? This will, coincidentally, also help you sleep better and longer at night. People who exercise are healthier, think more clearly, and may have delayed the onset of dementia. If that's not reason enough to stand up, that chair makes your butt look big.

If none of these ideas sound simple enough, start by breathing. I know it sounds so contrived and obvious. I used to feel silly doing it, even in the room by myself. Clearly, you are breathing all the time. The difference here is to be conscious of your breathing and what it can tell you. How we are breathing at the moment can help us recognize the specific feelings we are experiencing. When we are angry, our breath comes shorter and shallower. If we stop and lengthen and deepen our breath, we can feel some of the anger ebb and a little perspective flow into the open space inside of us. I call it the "10-4 Good Buddy." (Any

Smokey and the Bandit fans out there? No? Just me then.) Breathe in slowly for a count of four, pause for one second and then exhale slowly for 4 seconds. Do this ten times. You must really be patient on the exhale, and this is the hardest part and where we hurry. You will get better with practice. Set a time or appointment on your phone to remind you to consciously breath a few times a day and use this any time you are feeling a heightened level of emotion. This is an easy, natural and free place to start being healthier.

Demi-Chapter IV: Perfect

"On the whole, though I never arrived at the perfection I had been so ambitious of obtaining, … I was, by the endeavor, a better and happier man than I otherwise should have been had I not attempted it."

Benjamin Franklin

Remind yourself that it's okay to be imperfect. Well, golly. This is a loaded Demi-Chapter, isn't it? The struggle for perfection. Damned airbrushing. I completely blame our obsession with perfection on the airbrushed photo. As Meghan Trainor says in her fabulous song *All About That Bass* – "we know that s&%t ain't real, come on now, make it stop." The images we see every day make such an impact on us – even if we know that they are "digitally enhanced." This is a first world problem, but it is real and serious for the vast majority of us. When you walk ten miles a day to find clean drinking water you don't worry quite so much about if your butt jiggles when you walk or if people will laugh at your yard art. That said, it is still painfully real for many of us.

One of my guilty self-assurance pleasures, which is displayed prominently on my refrigerator, is a page from a lingerie catalog where this sweet young thing (seriously, she's barely fourteen) has this section of stomach that the air-brush missed. It's all folded and prematurely wrinkled skin and I LOVE IT! I mean, I hope that wasn't the end of her modeling career, but it gives me perspective. When I am feeling a bit chubby or wrinkly or – heaven forbid - *normal*, one glance at this photo reminds me that no one is perfect, and I don't need airbrushing. Mostly because I do not go out in public in my underwear.

Writing this section has forced me to think about my personal flaws. Lucky me. Let's compare our lives to writing this book. I am not worried about writing the perfect words in the first shot. I sit and write when I feel inspired and trust those words to be pretty good words. But I also know that I will reread and edit and revise this a dozen times before anyone else even lays eyes on them. But that's the rub, isn't it? We live our lives where people lay eyes on. If we could live out each day and then go back and revise our rather not-Mother-Teresa-like-moments, then perhaps we would be kinder to ourselves. But if we even compare ourselves to Mother Teresa, then aren't we setting unrealistic perfection goals? Yes, kind of, but my point is really that our fears about perfection are really fears that we can't go back and revise things before they become permanent. But this is life. I believe we were put on this earth to make mistakes and to learn to become better people, making the world better for others along the way. We were never designed to be perfect on this earth – never. I was married for 18 months. Yep. Not even two entire years. I used to regret that I wasn't a perfect wife, that I didn't try harder, that we didn't have a perfect marriage. But now I can remember the good times, I can remember that he is a good man and I know that no relationship is perfect. I can remember that we just weren't perfect for each other and I married for the wrong reasons. Relationships aren't perfect, and neither are we. When we let go of trying to be perfect, can be more real, more human, more content, and better people.

French Enlightenment philosopher, Voltaire, has a humanistic statement that I quite like: "perfect is the enemy of good." I'd say that perfect is the enemy of great. Great is somewhere between good and perfect. Striving for perfection distorts our ideas of contentment. In the third book of this series, the one about loving your life, there is a section that talks about your best life. Even your best life is still not a flawless life.

I waved the perfectionist flag for most of my life. Perfectionists tend to be their own worst critics. I was no different. It was only my renewed faith and my realization that there is little in my life that I truly control except my reactions and behaviors. That has helped me loosen up on my perfectionist tendencies. Now, I call myself a *sufficientist* when it comes to things outside of myself: things, trips, events. I've coined this phrase because I think it suits me nicely. A sufficientist is one who does some research, considers the options, then decides based on close enough, or sufficient. Once the decision has been made she gets on with her life being happy with her choice. A perfectionist must have exactly the right thing and struggles to be happy if she suspects that there might have been better out there. Sufficientists are not all willy-nilly. We have criteria, but once that criteria are met, then maybe we go with our gut or we like blue better than yellow or, for Pete's Sake just decide already! Perfectionists have criteria too, but they must find the optimal choice, they maximize and when they do this (if they ever get to a decision) then they often feel deep satisfaction that they chose exactly the perfect thing. The problem with being a perfectionist is that sometimes there is no perfect thing and happiness with a thing, event or choice can be elusive. Sufficientists often face criticism for giving up too early or settling for less than the best. To a sufficientist, the one they chose was the best choice for them at the time. They also, then, give themselves the gift of time and contentedness along with it. It is a fine line. A compromise. My partner, Will, is a perfectionist in some areas, but not all. He loves to do research and find the best product for the best price, but has a hard time deciding. I am a sufficientist and will perform an intense but brief bout of research and then decide. We are a great team because he will research and ponder for a year and then when I am ready to make a choice, he presents his findings to me (saving me the need to do heavy research) and then I choose the most sufficient one saving him the agony of choosing. It alleviates so much stress for both of us because he has informed a decision and guaranteed that the best choices are considered, and I have found a sufficient solution without spending too much time in the process. We are both happy and neither of us needs to be perfect.

Any math people in the house? No, don't run screaming from the room or throw the book on the fire. People should never say "I'm not good at math." I have been a math educator for twenty years and I'd bet you use math every day and probably use it just fine.

Anyway, I would like to call on a very fancy math word with a very simple concept. It is called an asymptote. An asymptote, in laymen's terms, is a value, represented by a line, that, an equation approaches but never reaches. Much like perfection. We get closer and closer and infinitely closer, but we will never, ever equal perfection.

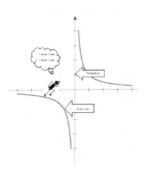

So, no matter how many times I revise this section of the book it will never be perfect. I will never be a perfect writer. I will never be a perfect anything. And neither will you. Why? Because it doesn't happen. Lives are too complex, and we are not meant to be perfect. To presume that we can be perfect on this earth is a tad arrogant, don't you think? Jenji Kohan, creator of *Orange is the New Black*, said that her words to live by are: "Flaws are in the eye of the beholder (Oprah, 2014)." Amen to that.

Many years ago, during a hike in the Rocky Mountains, I was contemplating an emotional reaction I had had earlier that week that left me feeling unsettled and grossly unattractive. At this point, I cannot even remember what it was, but I do remember feeling a heightened sense of worry over how others would see me. While sitting next to a stream, with my journal, it finally dawned on me that I am only a moderately observant person, but more so than most, and I rarely, if ever, notice things about a person physically that make any impact on my opinion of that person. If I don't see it in others, the chances that they even bother to notice it in me are quite slim. This was both humbling and enlightening. So, what if my hair is flat for the interview? If they notice it and it makes a difference, then maybe that isn't where I want to work anyway. Maybe I have put on a few pounds during the six months of working on this project. I dress pretty conservatively so if anyone even notices and thinks "boy is she letting herself go" well, that is their problem, right? I still need to remind myself of this occasionally when I am having a low-self-esteem day, but generally, my entire mindset of how others see me (and how I see others and myself) has changed thanks to this one moment by a stream in the mountains. Instead of always worrying about my weight and my hair I should instead remember that no one who matters is judging me. I am healthy (mostly), vital (generally), pain-free (kinda) and able (thankfully). Bobbi Brown, owner of Bobbi Brown Cosmetics, made a similar statement in 2014 that I love to recall: "If you look too closely, you're seeing imperfections that no one else is seeing but you. Truly, no one notices... Everyone is too busy with their own stuff."

Even if I saw myself as perfect,

someone standing right beside me might not see me as perfect. If she sees me as perfect, but I do not, am I still perfect? If I am perfect alone in a forest, but nobody sees it, am I still perfect? Should I strive to be my idea of perfect? My spouse's idea of perfect? The fitness magazine's idea of perfect? Your idea of perfect? As you can see, it is a dizzying concept. If your idea of perfect for you is a size 0 and I know that my bones, without muscle or fat, are actually larger than a size 0, then I can hardly see perfect for me as a size 0. The pursuit of perfection is perfectly maddening. You can be happy with who you are, how you look. Augusten Burroughs summed it beautifully by writing, "I myself am made entirely of flaws,   stitched together with good intentions."

You can have a satisfying day. You may even have a perfect moment. I will not try to define what a perfect moment would be.   Your perfect moment may involve squirrels or children or ice cream while all those things all may cause hives for someone else. If you did not have a perfect day, or a perfect moment or a perfect life, never forget that someone out there, looking in, thinks at least one aspect of your life is perfect. Guaranteed. I have worked with thousands of students, young adults, adults, and older professionals. The one thing I know is that we all have really excellent parts of our life. I met a middle-aged man once while serving Thanksgiving dinner to the homeless. At that time, I had no faith to speak of. This man, who had lost everything, had a miraculous faith and a smile that carried so much grace it could have stopped a train. Looking at me maybe he saw perfect health, wealth and charity. But looking at him, I saw perfect faith.

I remember distinctly the first day I recognized that an average day had been a great day. It was in the fall of 2013 – I was thirty-eight years old. The fact that I had not realized the greatness of an average day until I was thirty-eight almost makes me sad until I realize that some people never realize this possibility. Nothing great happened. It was an average day with a great attitude. I did not grumble or cuss or roll my eyes once. I laughed and felt perfectly content.

The next day was lousy. Some lousy things happened, and I let them be lousy. I wallowed in it like a hippo in a bog on a sunny day. I dove for the mud and rolled in it and *then* I realized that doing so made me muddy. Sometimes we revel in feeling bad. We take up the presidency of Martyrs-R-Us because our lives aren't perfect; sometimes we feel it for a minute, sometimes for years. Only we can stop that. Does it really feel good to wallow in bad feelings? Our lives aren't perfect. We aren't perfect. We forgive ourselves for our moment of wallowing and we move on. That's what I tried to do. I wallowed, vented, cried, pouted, did some online shopping therapy and then I stopped. I stopped and physically stepped away from the space I was in. I am not going to say that I handled it perfectly, whistled a happy tune like Mary Poppins or blue birds came and sat on my shoulder. The day was still a struggle. It was a struggle against my idea of perfection and what my perfect day should be. It was a struggle against my own internal negativity and perfectionism and that's a battle I can win (most of the time).

My whole point is this – define something more powerful than perfection for yourself. Happiness. Contentment. Peace. Being ulcer-free. Being perfect means accepting that neither you, nor your neighbor, nor your partner, friend, child, parent, the grocery store cashier, the airplane flight attendant – not one person on this earth can or ever will be perfect. Just the stress of perfection is paralyzing. Researchers report that those of us who have a greater number of stress points are more likely to develop dementia later in life. With all of the external stressors in our lives, do we need to voluntarily give ourselves another?

A colleague of mine works every day to wake up having a good day. She inspires me. I want to start the moment over if it isn't good. She is always positive. What happens to us is not what makes it good. It is how we handle it. You know that old cliché. But it is cliché for a reason. It's accurate. What exactly would happen if life was perfect? What would he say? What would she do? If everyone would get their act together, my life would be PERFECT! Or not. And that's ok.

Demi-Chapter V: Moderation

For life today in America ... involves not
only family demands, but community
demands, national demands, international
demands
on the good citizen, through social
and cultural pressures... This is not
simplicity but the life of multiplicity...It
leads not to
unification but to fragmentation.

Anne Morrow Lindbergh,

A Gift From The Sea

page 26, 1955

We don't have to do it all. I think
this is an American problem. The classic
over-achieving, first-world problem. The
quote above was written in 1955 – yes, my
friends, sixty years ago. It could have been

written yesterday. That shocks me and seems so terribly sad. Have we learned nothing? In fact, I think we have gotten much, much worse.

My dear friend is an Irish-born, naturalized American over-achiever. After stops all over the world she landed here, I think, because she can't sit still, and she fits the Colorado lifestyle just fine. She once told me that if you can't run a 5K after completing an all-day climb of a 14,000-foot peak then you have no business being on the mountain. Seriously. I can barely run a 5K if Satan is chasing me. She's not a fan of moderation. But I love her anyway.

We want so much fill-in-the-blank that it seems we need to do more and more. Recently I have been admiring those who simplify their lives. I have never before understood how some people can give up everything, move to a beach community and manage a rental storage unit business for the sheer pleasure of being near the beach. Once

I reached my late 30s, I understood that. If I may, I think the *new* American dream is now to give up everything, slow down and live a quiet, contented life. How else can you explain the tiny house phenomenon? It used to be embarrassing to live in a shed. Now it's hip! Ironically, there is still a negative image of those who slow down their lives. Stephanie Ponder, Editor for *The Costco Connection*, cited Journalist Carl Honoré, in her June 2015 article "Enjoy life more by doing less." He attributes our needed for constant busyness to the perception that "slow is a four-letter word indicating to American society that the person who is slow is lazy, unmotivated, unambitious, unproductive – all of the things that nobody wants to be (Ponder, 32)." Because of this, he hypothesizes, people choose not to slow down, prioritize, or just say no, even when they know it is the best choice for them. They feel guilt and shame about their value in this world where speed and productivity define value.

But, I urge you to look at how healthy people live in retirement. This is truly the heart's-content: downsizing, RVing around the country, moving to the mountains, starting a yoga class, learning to knit, filling the grandchildren with sugar and sending them home, spending the whole day on the patio reading a good book, golfing, playing tennis with friends, painting, exploring, creating. Could it be that I yearn for an RV? Crikey. When did that happen? These are the things that I dream about doing. But all of my life, at least since I was eleven, has been an endless to-do list. A good day is often a productive day. But on the days when the 117-item to-do list doesn't get done, I feel frustrated because only 111 are crossed off. I even add the things I did that weren't on the list and then cross them off just to feel better about myself. Oh, sure, you laugh, but there are a lot of us out there who do this. We take on one more thing because it is expected, because so-and-so does it, because it is what good moms, dads, girlfriends, wives, husbands, sisters, daughters, sons, friends or employees do. But does the one more thing make us happier?

Good intentions can lead to so much stress. Feeling obligated to help can lead to resentment. Remember that comment in Demi-Chapter I about my friend's birthday? Do you know what happened in 2013? I sent her an Amazon gift the day before her birthday, during a meeting, because I was supposed to do something thoughtful but hadn't gotten around to it yet. In 2015 I sent a card, thinking I would get her gift to her when she came to town the next month. Was it still a thoughtful gift, given a month late? It was an expectation I forced on myself. I didn't resent my friend for having a birthday, but sometimes I resent my dog for needing walked, my family for needing fed, or even, ridiculously, I resent Will when I choose to do something for him that _he never asked me to do_. How is this even remotely logical? It isn't. I am still overwhelmed by the things I have done to myself. We set expectations for ourselves that are unreasonable and then stress out when we don't meet the wholly unreasonable expectations no one cares about but us. Anyone else see the lunacy here?

Why do we do this? Why don't we just shorten the list? Why do we insist that it all has to be done, be done now and be done perfectly? Why not let something slide for today? What really must be done? What should be done? What really doesn't need to be done today?

I'm not suggesting you ignore a major health issue – this is not a license to make dangerous avoidance choices - but something small, like not doing the dishes before bed in exchange for snuggle time with your kids or lover? Martha Beck, author and life coach, suggests that you make a list of things you absolutely have to do, then look carefully at the list and ask yourself: "Is it absolutely true that you must do all of these things? Would you meet an untimely end if you didn't do them?" In a few pages, you will do an activity to help you prioritize your to-do list and find some moderation.

When I look back at my home growing up, I see a great example of this. Mom worked full time as a teacher, then came home, made dinner for the family of five, read to us over dessert, sat down to grade papers or do lesson plans or pay bills, watched a little t.v. with Dad and fell asleep in the recliner or in bed with an open book next to her. Notice house cleaning wasn't in that list. Our house wasn't Martha-Stewart-perfect. In fact, we kids did not do enough to help, and she was too tired to fight us on the point. Funny, my mom is actually more concerned about doing it all now than she was then. I see that now when my own very-nearly-step-daughters hate doing dishes too.

Mom made the choice that it wasn't a priority for her. Spending time with us, caring for us, preparing for her students the next day, and taking a few minutes to relax were her priorities. Clear kitchen counters? We got to that when company was expected. There was a time when I thought this was a failing on Mom's part. Boy, was I wrong! This was a brilliant survival tactic that produced tidy daughters with a whole lot of appreciation for Mom's model of priority making.

How many of us have the nerve to do what Mom did? Can you leave the counters dirty? In my spare time, I run a company whose entire purpose is to help people organize themselves so that life is simpler and the choices easier. I see that we kids should have helped more. I see that we could have gotten rid of some of our extra stuff, I see that we could have organized the house better so tidying and de-cluttering were easier, but we didn't. That was the choice

Mom made. And we all turned out just fine. When company comes over our houses look lovely.

I have helped Will raise three beautiful daughters, the aforementioned pseudo-step-daughters, through the "good grief" teen years. This has helped me see the value of instilling tidiness without neurosis. If the dishes aren't done – I can still go to bed and sleep wonderfully. The girls range in tidiness from "I'll clean when I can no longer see the floor" to an insistence on immaculate. I see it as my duty to help them see that clean is nice, but so is a nap.

I know so many women who drive themselves to complete breakdowns over cleaning the house, organizing the kids, working full time, preparing healthy meals, taking care of elderly parents, looking beautiful, and being everything to everybody. Men who work sixty to eighty-hour weeks to provide for a family they rarely get to see. Why do we do this?

What can we stop doing? What can we give ourselves permission to moderate? How do we rid ourselves of the guilt? Did you know that in 2011 about 57% of Americans left 70% of their vacation days unused (according to CNN, May 2016)? What is that all about? I have made a vow to take time off from work, slow down, make more manageable to-do lists and just sleep, vacation, take walks, write, and do things that are what I want to do and not "tasks" I've assigned myself. Number 47 on my list for today is to tell you how that's going.

Activity 1.5.1 Priority Squares

Adapted from Stephen Covey's *The 7 Habits of Highly Effective People*, 1989, The Time Management Matrix on page 151. If you find this activity helpful, I highly recommend reading Covey's book and especially the section on Habit 3.

Needs:

1. relatively quiet location for 2 hours (if you can't do this, find a safe place to store your work so you can return to it),
2. writing utensil with lots of ink/lead,
3. lots of 1.5" sticky notes (or pieces of paper and scotch tape) and a notepad with at least four sheets.

Steps:

1. Find a moderately quiet place in which to work.

2. Write down an exhaustive list of items that must be done, want to be done, and would be great to be done. Write each item on a separate piece of paper/sticky note. Keep them all separate but write until you cannot think of a single additional thing. This may be hundreds of things if you list "breakfast," which you should list if it weighs on you. I encourage you to list everything that you feel is important

enough to be taking up precious brain and emotional space. This is the longest and hardest part of the activity.

3.   Label each of the four sheets of paper with one of the four labels, representing the intersection of Importance and Urgency, as shown below.

- o   Important and Urgent
- o   Important and Not Urgent
- o   Not Important and Urgent
- o   Not Important and Not Urgent

Important	Not Important	
		Urgent
		Not Urgent

4.   Place your items onto one of the sheets. Here is a brief example of one of my grids.

Important	Not Important	
Important & Urgent ✞ Blood tests ✞ Pay electric bill ✞ Locate checkbook ✞ Call Mum about trip ✞ Replace spare key to hiding place	*Not Important & Urgent* ✞ Vacuum dog hair tumbleweeds from under the couch before guests arrive ✞ Complete report for Monday's meeting	**Urgent**
Important & Not Urgent ✞ Empty the dishwasher ✞ Dry cleaning ✞ Caulk the shed ✞ Paint the shed ✞ Send wedding gift	*Not Important & Not Urgent* ✞ File bills and receipts ✞ Sort through coupon file ✞ Schedule sewing class ✞ Put Barbie dolls on eBay	**Not Urgent**

What can you not do today? Tomorrow? This week? Be honest and real with yourself. "Clean countertops" may be important and not urgent. "Buy new running shoes" may be both important and urgent if you are starting a new training plan or are facing injury with your old pair. It may be not important and not urgent if you have six pairs in your closet that are perfectly fine. Those items that are not important and not urgent may be items on your list that can be delegated or just thrown away. Not urgent may become urgent eventually. Say when you put off doing dishes for so long that it becomes a hazardous waste site.

Tackle the Urgent/Important tasks first and rally people to help you. Paying the electric bill, fixing the broken lock on the front door, scheduling an appointment to get a suspicious lump examined might all be urgent/important items. Then move on to Urgent/Not Important items. These are the least fun, usually. I call this the necessary evil box. For me, these are obligations that I do not enjoy. Sometimes, though, this helps me to see what I consider obligations and to contemplate why they are obligations and whether or not they are important. This instant, I can't think of a single urgent/unimportant thing in my life right now. Yay me! Unless the 437 unread work emails count and then I am in trouble.

We often give ourselves obligations that actually aren't. For example, there is a sense of obligation around homemade cookies. "Make cookies for the new neighbors" can just as easily be "walk over to welcome the new neighbors and introduce our family." Who knows to what they are allergic or opposed to eating anyway? They will not think, "I can't believe that family came without cookies! What kind of neighborhood are we living in?" And if they do, their problems cannot be fixed with even the best Snickerdoodle.

Use this as a way to help you prioritize your list and your life. Once you complete the grid, you may want to come back to it weekly to add or remove items and regularly process your to-do list. You may find that, over time, undone Important/Urgent become Not Important/Not Urgent because the moment has passed. "Send dress to dry cleaners before Josey's wedding" in June may not be all that urgent or important now that it is October and you wore whatever was clean to Josey's wedding and not one person noticed.

One last note about moderation and that is what Merrilee Boyack, author of *Toss The Guilt and Catch The Joy*, calls "Problem Ownership and NMP – ('Not My Problem') (89)." Are there any NMP items on your list? Are you owning the problems of others? For example, our daughter, Claire, is going to college for her freshman year sometime in late August. Notice I said sometime in August. I do not know when. It is a few weeks away and she has yet to figure out what day moving-day is. So, I am reminding her to find out, so we can take the day off to move her. Technically, this is NMP. She's a big girl. If she has to move herself because she doesn't give us enough time to get time off work, well, that's her problem, right? Yes …. Sort of. It's her Dad's problem, I mean she isn't my kid, technically. Well… No. I am making it my problem because I want her move to college to be smooth and calm, so she starts this wonderful adventure on a positive note. Ultimately, this is our problem because if it is a disaster then it may change her entire first year, which may change our entire empty nest. But, technically, it isn't my problem. Still, I am choosing to own it, or at least a slice of it. My friend Malory is moving across the country in four days so that her husband can start medical school. It is a wonderful and exciting adventure for which they have yet to start packing. I am worried about this, but it is not my problem. I bought her packing supplies to get her started and I wished her well. As much as there is this little super-star inside me going, "oh, well, I will just go over and spend the day on Saturday helping her pack everything perfectly," I will not do this. I will go to the pool instead. This is not my problem and I cannot own it. She hasn't asked me to own it. I am saying no to my self-inflicted obligation and I am going outside to play.

Whatever you choose – give yourself permission to do it later or not do it at all. Carolyn Rasmus wrote in her book, *Simplify*, "the bottom line is that it is impossible to do everything, be everything, and meet everyone's expectations. That is an important lesson to learn. And, if you are like me, it is a lesson to be reminded of again and again." So, let's start now. It is okay to not do it all. Moderation in all things. Say it with me. "It is okay to not do it all. Moderation in all things." Ahhhhh, that feels better already.

Demi-Chapter VI: Do-overs

Any man can make mistakes, but only an idiot persists in his error.

Cicero

Life does have do-overs. Elizabeth Gilbert wrote one of my favorite books, *Eat, Pray, Love*, about her journey across the world to find herself. I read it every couple of years and it speaks to me differently every time. At one time in my life, I was contemplating a divorce and praying for a major career shake up. I was reading her book at the time. She says on page 115,

> "...when you sense a faint potentiality for happiness after such dark times you must grab onto the ankles of that

happiness and not let go until it drags you face-first out of the dirt – this is not selfishness, but obligation. You were given life; it is your duty (and also your entitlement as a human being) to find something beautiful within life, no matter how slight."

I love that quote. She is giving us permission to embrace the do-over. It turned out that I did get the divorce and I did hold onto the ankles of a glimmer of hope until it pulled me from the muck. I initiated an emotional do-over. I am now taking a serious look at changing a long career and scrambling desperately for a faint potentiality to latch onto. I need either a career do-over or an attitude do over. This book is a start. I found, after almost two decades in education, the profession I loved so dearly has changed drastically and the joy I felt is harder to find. This was my calling in life and now there is something else God has planned for me.

So now what? I need a serious do

over. Not that this career was a mistake, it wasn't you don't need a mistake to have a do-over. Sometimes you just want a do-over to do it a little better. Will and I instituted a do-over a few years ago. We had lots of back story, but we redefined who we are and where we are going. We hadn't made any real mistakes, we just needed to reevaluate. I changed my attitude. I got a grip on myself. We both sought help outside of ourselves. We initiated a do-over. This didn't involve changing each other. It involved changing ourselves and hitting the restart button. We came at our relationship with historical knowledge and a fresh perspective that we really wanted to make this work and we were the ones we wanted to grow old with. Our relationship is stronger than ever today, many years later.

Where do you need a do-over? If you can't think of a single area in your life that needs a do-over, congratulations! Skip to the next Demi-Chapter and come back when you do.

For the rest of you, is there anything about your life you would like to change? Improve? A conversation you want to have over again? Or perhaps a conversation you never had but really want to have? Now is your chance. Now is always your chance. Tomorrow is your chance too, but now is the best chance. You know that saying, "life isn't a dress rehearsal"? Well, it isn't a dress rehearsal, but it isn't closing night either. Yes, yes, doors close, doors open, doors revolve, doors hit us on the way out, but that doesn't mean you cannot start over.

I think there are times when do-overs are completely one-sided. For example, I can think of at least three times in my life when I have reached out with a letter to do over the way a friendship ended, even to find a long-lost half-brother. Do-overs may be best served in cursive. I'm just saying. The letters I wrote and sent were for me, not for the receiver. I have to be honest about that. I hoped that the letters would illicit a positive response, but none of them did, that I know of. Still, for me, they were all about doing it over and doing it kind, more maturely, more humbly, and more honestly. I have not seen or heard from my brother in decades, but I still hope he received the letter and knows I was thinking of him. I may never know if my letters made any impact or if they were received in the intent that they were sent, but for me, it was the do-over I needed.

Do-overs are the opportunity to start again, to try again. It could be revamping a healthy eating plan, an exercising plan, a relationship, a dream or to have a controversial conversation over with a better tone. I have dreamt of writing a book for about a decade. I have tried a few times, but the timing was not right. Not many of us can give up everything, get an advance from our publisher and travel the world, forsaking all grown-up responsibilities. Although, if there are any publishers reading this, I am game to give it a try! In the spring of 2013, after a soul-searching road trip to the Canyonlands in Utah, I gave myself a do over and I started outlining this book. Now, I am writing it. I was writing it while trying to work full time, battle newly discovered food allergies and health problems and reenergize my relationship with Will. I haven't implemented my do-over as dramatically as I thought I would, but I am closing in on this dream. Now, it is 2015 and I have reduced my work contract for a year to do this, get healthy and uncover the life I think is hidden under forty years of obligations. If I hadn't given myself another chance – a career mini do-over – I wouldn't have this opportunity to write and to start to work my way into the next life chapter. By the last Demi-Chapter, you may be reading that I quit my job and am writing from a tiny home on the beach.

Dale G. Renlund, cardiologist and leader for the Church of Jesus Christ of

Latter-Day Saints, reminded me that as we change, "we will find that God indeed cares a lot more about who we are and about who we are becoming than about who we once were." Even Nelson Mandela once said, "I'm not a saint – that is unless you think a saint is a sinner who keeps on trying." To me this means that we are encouraged to do over.

That is really the point of our life. If do-overs are God-given gifts, then it would be a rather silly thing to waste them. Each and every one of us can make a do-over of small or large proportions. No, life is not a dress rehearsal, but there is always another night and the show must go on.

Demi-Chapter VII: Forgiveness

You can't possibly climb up the mountain to a new life without unloading your knapsack of all the heavy stuff that has been weighing you down…It's best to travel light and dump the unnecessary baggage.

Joan Erikson

Live in the present; forgive your past. This Demi-Chapter goes hand-in-hand with the last. Life does have do-overs and the only way to truly embrace the do-over and live in the present is to forgive yourself and others for the hurt that is tarnishing your joy. We are so hard on ourselves. The expectations we set for ourselves are unrealistic and, often, overwhelming. We expect perfection from ourselves and others, leaving deep resentment, anger and sadness inside us that often hangs over us like a cloud, blocking our joy like a storm (see Demi-Chapter III: Perfection).

How do we move out from the shade and into the sun? Forgiveness. We all have to take time to reflect, forgive, and let go within the hustle and bustle of our every day. We have to have the courage to tell our loved ones that we need time and quiet and an opportunity to move out of the past and be in the present. For some this is taking a long bubble bath, for others it may be taking a long drive, for others it may be a week of solitude at a mountain yoga retreat, and some of us need years of support from mental and spiritual health advisors. Whatever it is, you must recognize what you need in order to forgive your past mistakes. When author and psychologist Martha Beck asked her readers what they wanted to give themselves for Christmas, they "responded with forgiveness and acceptance – freedom to accept both

what you've done and what you want to do –
without criticism or self-blame."

What are your hang-ups in life? What
do you struggle to forgive yourself or others
for? Is it your housework? Is it your
relationship history? Work? Lost friends?
Lost opportunity? Hurt pride? Regrets only
waste our time. We must learn from the
events of our lives and take those lessons
forward with us into the future, but the pain
can stay behind.

Many of the regrets, fear and pain of
the past are things we hold inside that deeply
impact our present even when we may never
speak of them to another soul. We feel
ashamed of our mistakes, embarrassed or
angry with ourselves. We fear if anyone else
knows of it we will be judged, or we will
damage current relationships. The most
important step is to identify how you will
forgive yourself, accept yourself as you were
and as you are now and take the step out of
the past and into the present. In

Shakespeare's *As You Like It*, Oliver, after repenting and creating himself anew, tells Celia and Rosalind, that the terrible man they describe to him "'Twas I, but 'tis not I. I do not shame to tell you what I was, since my conversion so sweetly tastes, being the thing I am." I adore this because I feel so akin to the sentiment. Regardless of your past mistakes, you can become something you are proud of. You can forgive yourself and embrace what you are becoming. You may need a good friend to help you. You may need a good therapist to help you. Whatever it takes, it is worth the time, effort, and money to make it happen.

Activity 1.7.1 Planning Forgiveness

1) *What haunts you from your past?* List anything you dwell on, think about more than once a year and feel miserable about when you do.

2) *For each item, identify the <u>feeling</u> attached (anger, fear, regret, sadness, etc.).*

3) *One at a time, consider the event and the feelings, and answer these questions:*

    a. *What can I do about this now to make it stop? Is it an external or internal action?*

    b. *Is there any part of this I still control?* If you cannot impact it, then you are letting it control you.

    c. *What am I willing to do?* Take an action or let it go.

    d. *How and when will I do it?* Take your first step.

At 33, I took my life into my own hands. Who says aging is not worth every penny? I did a lot of journaling. I did counseling. I was brutally honest about myself and past relationships. I joined a church I believe in. I wrote my parents a letter (seriously?!) and told them all the background of my divorce that I never told them.

I was honest with my doctor, with my friends, with my church. I went back and burned all my journals from all of the years of relationship foolishness. Having been overweight most of my life and desperate to be seen as beautiful I had entwined myself in relationships that weren't good for me, with men who didn't respect me or care about who I was, but only what I could do for them. They weren't relationships that taught me anything at the time, they were only impactful in retrospect when I examined the dark underbelly of each monster. I felt pity for the sad little girl I had been. I forgave myself. I let go. It was cleansing and necessary for me. It has taken me years and I would be lying if I said I did not occasionally yearn to relapse into self-loathing over those mistakes, but now I can see it coming and I can resist it. And I accept who I was, why I was, who I am now, and why I will never go back to being that sad girl, desperate to be loved, desperate to matter. And, more and more, I expect those who love me to accept me for who I am. Now, on the knife's edge of forty, I like myself better than I ever have. My dear friend, Catalina, told me that she finally found her confidence at forty. She loved forty. Jennifer Aniston did, too. If a Hollywood paparazzi darling can love turning forty, then I can. I am pretty awesome. I bet you are too. Unfortunately, you can't feel completely free self-love until you can forgive yourself and others and embrace your present.

Is there a hurt, from your recent or distant past that you just cannot seem to let go of? Are you allowing someone else to control your happiness by holding onto the hurt that they caused? Maybe you are completely justified in your hurt, but withholding forgiveness only hurts you –

they do not pay any price at all. You and your family pay all of the costs. Eroding resentment and endless begrudging change who we are. I try to make forgiveness an act of mercy. I try to understand what motive was behind the hurt and I try to humanize the offender. I try to feel pity and understanding and then I work on forgiveness.

Will's mother is a kind and generous woman who absolutely despises me. I am guessing that this is out of fear that I will usurp her role as matriarch of the family, but she hasn't made her reasons clear to me. She desperately needs to be needed and the thought that she may not be needed is devastating to her, creating resentment, jealousy, and changing who she is on the inside. On Christmas Eve, 2010, after almost two years of holidays and Sunday lunches, she summarily uninvited me to everything because, in her view, these occasions were "for family." For many years, I was hurt and resentful and did not understand what I had done to merit this treatment. The truth was that I hadn't done anything except love and care for her son and granddaughters. I allowed this anger and resentment to ruin my Sundays and holidays for years and years – digging into the wound, reopening the wound, pouring salt in the wound.

I caused myself such unforgiveable pain because, in my pride, I wouldn't forgive her. For a few weeks I was furious at Will and hurt that he wouldn't confront her. But then I realized, I cannot ask him to shirk his responsibility to his mother or I would be acting with no more class than her. It wasn't his fault that she asked him to choose between her and me. It was also not fair for me to ask him to choose between her and me. She was putting him in the middle, putting the girls in an awkward position. I would not do the same to them. My own pride was the cloud hanging in front of my joy – not her actions, but my own.

On Christmas 2014, I finally let her go. I forgave myself for the wasted emotions, the resentment and the shame I had felt. That year I verbalized that I felt sorry for her. She was robbing herself of my company and my generosity, and her family wanted to spend less time with her because of her decision. I felt pity that she had to be so miserable. I felt truly sorry that this woman could not see all of the love her family had for her; she could not see her own worth. She causes herself and her family so much pain. That year I forgave her.

I spent the day volunteering at the animal shelter, snuggling and giving treats to the lonely animals. I smiled, laughed and made a difference in the lives of dogs who needed love. I felt the love of Christ in my heart and was able to spend the evening with my family after they spent the day with her. I understood that forgiving her and understanding her was my way forward. I learned to share my family with her. Even though I know that she thinks her son shouldn't love me and that I don't deserve to be in the lives of her granddaughters, I know that she is wrong and that I love her family well. I forgive her, I pray for her, and she can't hurt me anymore.

Activity 1.7.2 Giving Forgiveness

You will need a quiet and comfortable place to sit by yourself for this activity. Sit comfortably. If there is a window or outdoor space, that might be nice, but not needed.

Say the name of a person and the offense you wish to forgive. Hold the words in your hands like a bird or a butterfly. Let the feeling of forgiveness – not anger, shame, fear or hurt – fill you up. Say out loud, "*Name*, I forgive you for *offense*, and I let it go." Open your hands and release the bird to the air.

Example: "Jackie, I forgive you for

seeking love first from others before loving yourself. I let it go." Repeat this for yourself and others as many times as you need to. You may feel physically lighter after completing this activity.

But let's say you aren't at a place to be so benign (or don't have the desire to spend four years getting there). Can you still find the peace of forgiveness? Try this mantra to work through the early steps of forgiveness for your own sake: "[_____] *is not worthy of one more ounce of my energy. I am going to spend my energy on the people I love and care about.*" I still use this when talking myself through the hijinks of Will's mom and it does help me reach a more peaceful resolution when she introduces some new bitterness into the situation.

There is no reason to wait. Dig in. It won't be easy or painless, but once the grief and pain of the past are gone and you don't live back there with them, the world is a brighter place.

Demi-Chapter VIII:
Let go

In the end, only three things matter: how much you loved, how gently you lived, and how gracefully you let go of things not meant for you.

Buddha

Learn to let go. Okay. Now we know that we don't have to be perfect, we can leave some things undone and take every opportunity to make the most of our lives. We can take as many do-overs as we need. We should forgive and forget our pasts and embrace our present and future.

But how? When speaking of forgetting our past, we have to address letting go. It is so hard for humans to let go. My dog, Echo, takes a toy, buries it and forgets about it. If she finds it again it is like Christmas – she has already moved on. She can let go.

She embraces her fondness for shiny, distracting things and doesn't spend a second more than necessary on anything.

Here is a small list of items of which humans struggle to let go:

- **Of things.** Americans have a lot of stuff. Our houses, yards, cars, desks, stores and landfills are filled with stuff. We have a reality TV show dedicated to hoarders. Martha Beck advises, "The space that remains when we get rid of things, rather than accumulating them, offers a sense of luxury you might have thought came only from granite countertops." I love Martha Beck. Almost as much as I love my shoe collection.

- **Of regrets.** The truth is, you have never truly been in control of anything. Maybe you can wish you had done one thing instead of another, but you did not, and you can never know what your life would be like if you had. Rather than regret, and second guess yourself, the best question to ask is: How can I respond as gracefully as possible to whatever occurs and trust that I made the best choice I could have made at the time? I had perms put into my hair for fifteen years. Hours and hours of curlers and stinky solution. I could regret that, but I have let go of those regrets. I could die in a car crash tomorrow. If I was lying on the highway, I don't want my last thoughts to be of regrets of giant curly 1990s hair.

• **Of lost love and pain.** Persian poet and mystic, Jalal Al Din Rumi, who lived in the swinging 1200's, reminds us, even now, that "our task in this life is not to seek for love, but to merely seek and find all the barriers within ourselves that we have built against the love in our lives." Fear of hurt and fear of failed love team up to make the Berlin Wall of barriers. Time to tear it down.

- **Of pride.** We are taught from any early age not to embarrass ourselves or anyone in our near vicinity. Failure, mistakes, and the accompanying disappointment all spring from our expectation of an ideal outcome and our need to be accepted by others. I'm not saying that some pride isn't helpful – it often keeps us from drinking too much and skinny dipping in the neighbor's pool. Pride can get in the way when it keeps us from trying new things. We feel that we have to be an expert at something in order to put it on exhibit. I resisted fish on Lake Powell with my sister and her husband because the fear of mortification that would come with getting my fishing hook stuck in someone's face. No seriously. Have you seen that happen? It is gory and traumatizing and impossible not to laugh at. I only want to be laughed at when I mean to be funny. And I certainly don't want to hurt anyone. Plus, I knew that I super-suck at fishing and have no interest in touching a fish. Nonetheless, I gave it a try. Three whole entire days were spent fishing with no hook-face incidents. I even caught a few and dehooked a few (which required touching it – note: wear gloves, the scales are sharp and unpleasant). So, here is my challenge for you and me: let go of your belief about having to be an expert and just let yourself experiment like a child again. If we fail, so what? Have you ever watched a young child who has yet to be tainted by our society's fiercely competitive compulsion and desperate need to be perfect? He or she will play and play and play until they get it right. They might ask if they are doing it right, but if we say no that just keeps them wondering and trying. They aren't yet aware of the "if I can't get it the first time I am not going to try" mentality. I am not sure I was that child. As the youngest I think I always felt I had to prove myself. I had to not repeat my sister's "mistakes" (whatever those were) so I wouldn't do things I didn't think I could do well. If I could not compensate for lack of talent with effort, then I wasn't interested. For instance, I never learned how to roller skate/rollerblade/skateboard/ski or do anything that required a sense of balance and something between my feet and the ground. I was well aware of the possibility of my own death, even as a child, and I have never been a big fan of hurting myself. Mostly I did not want to look stupid, or clumsy, or, heaven forbid, have someone think I was fat, incompetent or needy (like if I did fall down and needed someone to help me up). What I see now is how much fun I have missed out on. Watching Will on his skateboard while I walk the dog, a part of me wishes I had learned. The other 93% of me still reminds me that I can break, and it will hurt a lot, and now I am more terrified of that than anything. With my pride issues, I'm still afraid of failing when it comes to physical activity and financial risks. I'm a Leo, after all. We are proud folk.

• **Of making sure everyone else is happy.** My friend, Joanne, once told me that I have an old soul. I liked the compliment. Now my old soul is finding a way to say, "that's your problem." This past Spring at Disney World, instead of feeling like it was my responsibility to ensure everyone's perfect vacation, I let our middle daughter take the lead at the Magic Kingdom and I, who had never been to any Disney park except Epcot, just wandered blissfully behind them, gawking at everything with wonder and smiling like the village idiot. I did not worry about looking like a 40-year-old child or losing track of them or missing out on something that they might have said or done or seen, or even if they were having a good time. I just lost myself in the moment. I utterly failed as tour guide and vacation Mom, but I had a marvelous time and I learned that it was totally ok. I left my "is everyone having a great time?" with the car in Simba 2.

- **Of anger.** Anger is rooted in fear, hurt, resentment and is completely 100% your problem. Identify the root of your anger and let it blow away. Angry that you were passed up for a promotion at work? Are you angry or hurt because you feel unrecognized and undervalued? Are you frustrated with yourself because you applied for the job, but then came in late every day this week and feel you made yourself look bad? Most of our anger is unfounded – or founded entirely with ourselves. One weekend we were in a car driving along the pacific coast in Manhattan Beach, California. We happened to have a professional driver at the time, arranged for us by the company we were working with that weekend. In front of us were two young girls on bikes. They were riding along, taking up the lane and clearly looking for which turn to take to get to the beach. Our driver became furious with them. Why? We weren't in a hurry. She was being paid by the hour. It was a beautiful day. I don't know the source of her anger, but I found it ridiculous and made a note to myself to practice patience instead of anger when I am behind the wheel. When I get angry behind the wheel it is 1) almost entirely my fault because I left the house late and now feel rushed to get where I am going, thus increasing my stress by being impatient with people who happen, to their misfortune, to be on the road with me; and 2) fear that I may be hurt. That's it. Neither are productive. Let the anger go.

- **Of resentment.** Acknowledging bad feelings to yourself (and sometimes others) allows those feelings to go away. When I can, I stop myself and say I am feeling resentful right now and I don't want to – it doesn't make sense to use my energy this way. That little ten-second step allows me to let it go. Sometimes it doesn't stay away, but it gives me a reprieve. I have heard it said that negative thoughts should be plucked like a weed. It may grow back, but for the time being it is done away with. The most important part of this is that resentment is a hateful, rotting pit that grows inside of us. When you compromise the mechanism inside you that sets you straight, you create resentment inside of you. When you ignore or shut down that mechanism to make someone else feel better or to save yourself difficulty, you end up causing yourself a lot of heartache (resentment!) and this just eats away at your happiness.

- **Of your job**, if it causes any of the previous six feelings. If you are burnt out at work, be honest with yourself about it. Try to identify what burnout looks like for you. Your health and the health of the relationships with people you love may depend on it.

- **Of that moldy stick of cream cheese** that you were once going to make into something glorious. I bet whatever you made (or bought!) was enjoyed and spent less time on your thighs.

- **Of grown-old dreams.** A wise man you might know named Professor Dumbledore, once advised, "It does not do to dwell on dreams and forget to live." My sister wanted to be a racehorse jockey when she was little. She is now 5'7" and we all weighed at least 120 pounds by middle school, so that dream was one she had to let go of. If she spent each day pining away at her dream of riding in the Kentucky Derby, she would probably be wasting precious time instead of raising two wonderful children.

- **Of Jealousy.** Even if green is a good color for you, getting there by way of soul-devouring jealousy is not recommended. It is hard for us to not constantly compare ourselves to others – our society practically demands it. But this is a good goal to take on. Are you happy with who you are? Your life is about you and no one else. In book two we will take a long hard look at how we love others. For right now, every time you feel that jealous monster whispering negative thoughts in your ear, I dare you to stop and immediately think or write or say out loud, one of the blessings of your life. Use something you are proud of or something you know you do well (not compared to others, just compared to you and your former selves). You never know what the person you are jealous of feels inside or struggles with. Replace it with compassion.

- **Of "fat pants"** you keep just in case. Granted all the cool kids will be wearing them in about three years when the fashion cycle comes back around, but you won't need them then either.

- **Of "skinny pants" you keep** – for what? Motivation? Sentimentality? Self-torture? I heard a story this weekend about a woman who had to be cut out of her jeans because they were so tight her feet went numb. That's reason enough for me. I will forever wonder if I will need to be cut out of my skinny pants if I ever tried to wear them again. Plus, by the time they fit properly, they will be totally uncool.

- **Of that such-n-such so-n-so gave you** – when? You can't remember but it's chipped, so you just use it to hold pencils.

- **Of 45-year old onesies**. Seriously, it happens. A friend told me his mom still had his first onesies in a closet.

- **Of the photo album** that was actually ruined in the great basement flood of 1978 and smells eye-wateringly musty but has a few pages that kind of dried flat so dear Great Grandma Amanda doesn't look quite as sallow and bloated as her sisters on the opposite page. This does no one any favors. And if your Grandma Amanda is anything like mine was, she'll come back and haunt you for wasting time thinking about it when you should be leading the mule-drawn plow across the field.

- **Of the faux zebra fur platform mules** with fluffy ostrich feather and purple accents from that groovy summer you graduated (or was it a Halloween costume?). Self-explanatory, I think.

- **Of tax returns from 1981.** The IRS and tax experts suggest keeping ten years of tax returns for reference. If, like me, your taxes have been moderately easy, and these are all nicely tucked into a single filing box, then you may be able to keep a few more. If each year takes up three boxes, then consult with your tax expert and start shredding. Never, ever, put important financial documents in recycling or trash, regardless of the age. Public service announcement from me to you.

- **Of old love letters** from some guy or gal you swooned over when you were 12. And don't try to find him/her on Facebook. If you are meant to be together, God will make it happen. If you are not, Facebook stalking will not improve matters.

- **Of the toaster oven that you thought you donated two house moves ago.** Donate it now.

- **Of fights with your mom or dad.** Besides being emotionally draining these can be permanently damaging. It never hurts to remember that they, or you, could be gone tomorrow and the only way anyone wants to be remembered is with love.

- **Of fights with anyone.** See above.

- **Of the name of the professor** who gave you your first and only C (bastard!). I'm still working on this one. Of course, maybe I am done because I cannot recall his name.

- **Of the boycott of the guy** at the deli who asked how long your daughter, who is actually your older sister, will be staying with you. He was just trying to be nice. This is why I don't talk to strangers, just in case.

- **Of finding self-value in the value others give you.** Just because you can do something, doesn't mean you should. Do you do more out of obligation, or a need to feel useful and valuable? Don't forget that you are the leader of your life and you can choose to believe and do what you want. If you want to be valued, start valuing yourself and let go of your worth in the eyes of others. That is their problem, not yours.

- **Of the plan you think you have for yourself.** God/The Universe has a plan;

try to tune in to that.

- **Of the belief that if you don't do it all and perfectly**, you are in some way a failure in your life, you are irrelevant. We run at such frenetic pace in our lives, we are bound to do something at 99% at some point. Or even 87%, 54% or 23%. I often connect my worth to my to-do list. I struggle with the idea that my relevance and importance are not tied directly to my productivity. Do you? Balderdash. You are relevant. Even if today you are just sitting on the patio reading this book. You are *very* relevant to me, thank you. I am buoyed by the news that our younger generation (and some us middle agers) are embracing the culture of living over the culture of doing and having and running.

- **Of telling those little white lies to cover your ass.** Honesty really is the best policy and it takes less energy.

- **Of believing that everyone needs to do** what you need them to do at exactly the time that you need them to do it. Nagging and yelling and whining and punishing doesn't work. It just makes everyone, including you, feel crappy. Tasks don't need to be done on your schedule. Will and I had a mostly effective system while the girls were growing up (as effective as any system is with three teenage girls in the house). We would give the girls a chore list, all the chores rotated, and they had until Saturday night to accomplish the chores. If they didn't, then they did not have weekend plans. We did not care when it got done, so long as it got done. This mostly worked, and the girls kept each other accountable. It was also a relief to us that we did not have to fight with the girls on Sunday night to make sure everything was done for the week.

- **Of stress.** It may be tough to get away from all of the stress in our lives, but we can deal with what we have and work to avoid intentionally taking on more. The result is a strong, healthier, more youthful and purposeful you. Like with any exercise, you may seem tight and only able to do a little, but with practice you become flexible and strong. It is the same for alleviating stress. According to the Institute for Health Metrics and Evaluation (http://www.healthdata.org/), as reported in the Texas Tribune in April 2012, from 1989 to 2015, the life expectancy of women, while increasing on average over the world, increased only 2.7 years compared to men's increase of 4.6 years (Murphy, B.). If this isn't a sign that we need to chill out, ladies, there will never be one.

That was a fun list. How do we know

when it is time to let go? I will use my own example. I mentioned earlier that I am revisiting my career path after twenty years and only one profession. I am slightly terrified. But here I sit, writing. When I thought about letting go I was hit with a biblical-parting-of-the-skies-and-chorus-of-angels-like-clarity that came out of my mouth more like, "well, nuts, I need to quit my job." Luckily, I did not draft the resignation letter that day, because I enjoy eating and am fond of the electric light, but I started on the path of letting the job, and possibly, the career, go. Here are the red flags that tell you to walk away (from anything, not just a job):

1) You feel like you are fighting an uphill battle [every day].

2) You feel obligated, not excited, to stay.

3) You do not feel valued.

4) Fear is holding you back.

5) You feel that you are compromising

yourself.

Okay, great, now what? How do we let go? For some stuff, I think fire is a nice separation technique. This does not apply to people or places of employment – even if they take your red stapler. Recycling (just remember to shred important documents with important personal information) and donating works, too. Marie Kondo suggests that you "keep only those things that speak to your heart. Then take the plunge and discard all the rest." You may need to recruit a friend who is willing to tell you that it is time to let it go. It will be easy for him; it isn't his stuff and he doesn't care what it is. Free up space, literally and figuratively. Let it go.

Activity 1.8.1 The Friendly Pragmatist

Consider some of the most common worries when it comes to letting go. In this activity, you will need to channel the spirit of the most pragmatic person you know.

Let's call the helpful person Peggy or Patrick. Think or write down the "What ifs" that keep you from letting go. Then ask Peggy Pragmatist what her response would be. Really hear her voice. What will she tell you? Here are some starters (add as many extra rows as you need):

What if... (examples)	Peggy/Patrick Pragmatist's Response (examples)
What if I need it later?	When was the last time you used it? If it was 1983, you don't need it.
What if it is worth something?	Take the time to find out what it's worth or get rid of it. It may not be worth your time, mental energy or rent on the space.

What if the kids want it?	Ask them.
What will I fill that giant hole of negativity with?	Something positive.
What if I forgive him/her, what will I hold against him?	Nothing. Just enjoy your sandwich.
What if what she said is true?	Do you believe it is true? If yes, then take some time to reflect on what that means for you. If no, then forget it.

What if she still doesn't forgive me even after I ask her to forgive me?	It is now entirely her problem.

What if my friends come over and notice that the thing, they gave me that I hate is no longer on display in my house?	You tell them that you really appreciate their thoughtfulness, but you are trying to let go of extra things and keep only the things that you really love – like them (and your sanity).
What if I can't find another job?	You should plan your exit strategy and have your financial plan in place before you quit.
What if I end up alone?	Alone is a state of mind. You have friends and once you are happy you will draw admirers to you, or it won't matter as much as you think. Or you might even like the time to yourself.
What if I give up control and then am unhappy with the results?	Giving up control means being happy with the outcome, whatever it might be. Expect to be happy, not unhappy.

What if... (Your turn)	Pragmatist's Response (Your turn)

Take it in small steps and celebrate each time you let something go by affirming how freeing it feels.

Demi-Chapter IX: Promises

Promise: a: a declaration that one will do
or
refrain from doing something specific.

Merriam Webster Online Dictionary

Keep the promises you make to yourself. I think the value of the promise has waned. It has become trite and overused in our 21st century self-fest. People throw out the word without really considering the implications. Like the word, "sorry," which is now the substitute for "you are upset, and I want you to stop being upset without my really having to own anything or think about it." "I promise" has become "if it is convenient and I remember then I will do this thing for you." This applies to promises we make to ourselves and to others.

From interviews, reading, and my own experience, the most common promises that adults make to themselves are: I will…

Travel the world

Write a book

Take a nap

Meditate

See that movie

Learn a language

Take a class in _____

Never take no for an answer

Never say yes when I mean no

Lose 10 pounds

Never go to happy hour when I just don't want to

Allow an impulse buy

Don't allow an impulse buy

Tell my parents I love them

Bake cookies and give them all away

Go somewhere and just sleep

Give up cigarettes

Come out of the closet   Start my own
business

Be honest with a friend

Donate to charity

Rescue a lonely pet

Admit that COMBOS are the best road
trip food ever created (this isn't a
promise as much as just something
everyone should do)

Just be who I am. (Don't forget that
there is an "I" in happiness.)

So, what does it mean to keep a
promise to oneself? Is there a time limit? Can
you keep a promise you made to yourself
decades ago? Of course! Heck, Hollywood
has been making money off of that concept
since the dawn of film. I propose that some
promises have expiration dates, but most do
not. My friend, Joanne, read my manuscript
and jotted this note in the margin: "I made a
promise to myself many years ago that I
would jump out of an airplane. Years came

and went, and I never did it. Finally, in 2014, for my 70th birthday, I kept that promise to myself. I went skydiving! It's never too late." How true!

Let's say that for twenty-one years you have been promising yourself that you are going to thank Aunt Pam for the graduation gift in 1993. If you are seriously still thinking about that, then do it. Keep that promise to yourself and get it off your list. You may end up mending a fence you did not even know was broken. If your promise to yourself involves someone who is deceased, then you might just have to be a little more creative in how you keep that, but it doesn't mean you have to abandon the promise. Possibly you made a promise to do something that requires physical strength that you no longer have. With modern advances and technology, you might still be able to keep that promise. Look into it. If not, then give yourself permission to change the promise to a more accessible one or let it go. Put the promise on your Priority Squares (Activity 1.4.1) and then move it to the Not Urgent/Not Important list and eventually throw it away.

But let's look at the promises you still have rattling around in your noggin'. Pick one. What is standing in your way? What are the reasons you have not done it? What are the root causes behind those reasons? What is one small step you can do today to keep that promise? Who is impacted that you need to talk to? What is a reasonable deadline? How can you remind yourself daily about your promise? What is your support system? You are going to work through all of these questions in the next few pages, but I want to walk you through them first with an example from my own life with explanations so when you go to look at your own promises, you can follow the example for support. The questions you will answer are in bold. My answers follow. The text is italics are note to you.

Activity 1.9.1 Promises, Promises *An Example*

Start small if you want but listen closely to your heart. What promise have you made to yourself that you really want to keep?

Promise to myself: write a book

I would like to keep this promise to myself because: I feel that I have a lot to offer others and I need to have my true voice heard. I need to feel like I am making a difference.

Five reasons I have not kept this promise to myself are: *Be honest with yourself. What is standing in your way? What are the reasons you have not done it? This list is for your eyes only. Don't judge, just write.*

1) I'm not sure that I have anything to write about.

2) I'm afraid no one would want to read it.

3) I have no idea how to get published.

4) It seems like one of those things everyone dreams about, but no one does once they are in a career.

5) I do not make time in my life with career, relationships and other obligations.

The Root Causes Behind My Hesitation

The root causes may be the hardest part of this activity. This is the dig-deep honest truth. Why didn't you do this? You may see that the same root cause manifests itself behind many different reasons. Notice in my example that the real root cause is fear of failure, masked as all kinds of other things.

The root cause behind reason 1) is: I only know education. Who wants to hear from me about life? Do I need to write a heavily researched book, or can I just write from my heart? I think writing takes a lot of research. I'm afraid I won't do it well.

The root cause behind reason 2) is: I believe that I am not a good storyteller. Numerous boyfriends have told me so and I have lost confidence in my ability to be interesting. I believe that most people do not get my humor and I want to make people laugh as they heal. I'm afraid it will be boring.

The root cause behind reason 3) is: I hear all of these horror stories about publishing companies and it sounds like it will take a ton of work and heartbreak. What if I write and no one wants it? What if I fail to get published? I will have wasted my time.

The root cause behind reason 4) is: I find lots of other things to do because I am afraid to put in all the effort and fail. It seems wasteful to dedicate all of my "spare time" to writing when I could be exercising or spending time with loved ones. I haven't found my passion yet.

The root cause behind reason 5) is: If I really wanted to do this, I would have majored in literature or journalism. I don't have the writing skills and now I am well passed the starving writer phase of my life. You hear about the accountant who becomes a best-selling writer in his 50s, but statistically, how often does that really happen? How can I give up my full-time job to write? I am afraid to be poor, unemployed, homeless, and unsuccessful.

Moving Forward

This is the hardest part for me. I know what I want to do and why I am not doing it, but how do I move forward? What little thing will I make time for?

What is one small step you can do today to keep that promise? Keep a list of potential topics in my phone or journal, collect articles and resources as I read them. Research publishing – can I do it on Kindle or Amazon or do I need a big publishing house?

Make a Plan

What risk am I willing to take to keep my promise? How can I swallow my pride and ask for help? How do I set aside time to finally make this happen? I answered these truly as I worked through this process and this book. Your answers are your own.

Who is impacted that you need to talk to?
Will. If I do this, I will spend less time focused on him. Maybe my boss – does he need to know? It won't impact my work – or will it? Do I quit my job to write? I could use the support if I try to do it while working. My parents - I still feel that I need to keep them informed, almost their approval.

What is a reasonable deadline? How many years will it take to write? My sister said I can self-publish on Kindle in sections so maybe I can get started without having to write the whole thing at once. I would like to set aside two hours per week to write. I'd like to have it drafted in a year.

How can you remind yourself daily about your promise? Keep a sign on my refrigerator, keep time set aside in my weekly calendar, keep my writing file visible on my desk at home.

What is your support system? My friends

will support me – how can I ask them to proactively encourage me? My sister has helped me talk through the whole process. Will respects my interest in doing this. We have talked about taking a break from my career to write but that terrifies me. Can I really take that much risk?! Can I let go of my independence and rely so heavily on Will? I will tell people I trust that I am doing this, so they ask about it and keep me motivated.

Activity 1.9.2 Promises, Promises: It's Your Turn

What promise has haunted you for so long that it absolutely needs to be addressed? Grab a pen and do this same activity on the next page. You may not know all of the answers the first time. You may need to come back to it. That's alright, just do it.

Promise to myself:

I would like to keep this promise to myself because:
_____

Five reasons I have not kept this promise to
myself are:

1) _____
2) _____
3) _____
4) _____
5) _____

The root cause behind reason 1) is:

The root cause behind reason 2) is:

The root cause behind reason 3) is:

The root cause behind reason 4) is:

The root cause behind reason 5) is:

What is one small step I can do today to
keep that promise?

Who is impacted that I need to talk to?

What is a reasonable deadline?

How can I remind myself daily about my promise?

What is my support system?

Don't be afraid to keep your promise. And keep it now. You deserve it.

Demi-Chapter X: Instincts

Don't let the noise of others drown out your own inner voice. And most important, have the courage to follow your heart and instincts.

Steve Jobs

Trust your instincts. I like to call this the "Damn, I knew it" effect. Are you familiar with that feeling that you did not do something your gut told you to do and then really, really wish you had? This happens when we second guess our instincts or when something gets in the way of our following our instincts. Instinct goes by many names. I call it The Spirit. Everyone calls instinct something – the Universe, 6th Sense (Do you see dead people?), little fairies on my shoulder, ego, intuition, gut, heart. Whatever you call it – you have to learn to hear it, trust it, and then do something about it or you'll end up running through the woods in stilettos in a horror movie.

Here we find fear showing up again. Why do we not follow our instincts? Why do we not step into the dark? We take the rational, sometimes safer, route. While we often hear stories of instinct saving our physical lives, our instincts can often urge us to go to a place of emotional risk. We see that going there may lead to something scary – failure, financial or emotional risk – so we don't do it. We don't see the learning that is meant for us that we will miss. Our instincts can often answer questions that have been plaguing us. Should I go? Should I stay? Should I do that? Should I not? When we do not know what to do, what decision to make, we hope for our instincts to take over. And they will. When we have asked all the questions, done all of the research, said all the prayers, sought all the council and cannot make a choice, our instincts can help us. If we trust them.

Our instincts encourage us to do (and often clarify for us) what's right for us, even when others disagree. Prayer is powerful and may help clarify what we should do next, so long as we act. Dallin H. Oaks, an American attorney, jurist, author, professor, and religious leader, reminded me in an article in August 2013 that, "we will get promptings of the Spirit when we have done everything we can, when we are out in the sun working rather than sitting back in the shade praying for directions on the first
step to take."

Sometimes our instincts show us the long view and we have to start working out the details. There is something deep inside me that told me that I would write; I first got this impression in my teens. I thought journaling would be enough, but it wasn't. I thought professional writing might do the trick, but after three articles, I've learned that writing about math education doesn't completely satisfy that call (imagine that). My Spirit is telling me that I am meant for more. Part of following my instincts is acknowledging that and sorting out how to make it happen. Oftentimes our instincts are just reminding us of our dreams. When we need it to, it steps up and redirects our path, gives us little hints, and provides us with messages that, if we are in-tune, can move us in the right direction. If we stubbornly insist that we know what is best and ignore our instincts, then we will miss a lot of opportunities. It is like driving in a roundabout. Instinct is the sign that says get off here, but if we ignore it we just go around and around until we see it and eventually head in the right direction. When we were travelling in Lisbon, Portugal, the wonderfully helpful gentleman at the rental car station was giving us directions for finding the highway south. Bless his cotton socks if he did not tell us, "If you miss the exit, it's a small town, you'll get it the next time around." I think this is actually great advice for life. If you miss it the first time around, you'll get it the second time. It's a short life.

Those who are in-tune trust their instincts and get headed in the right direction while the rest of us go around and around. The next time you might get off at the right exit while that other guy is going around and around. I am not sure that anyone has ever completely trusted instincts every single time and therefore avoided the roundabout. It doesn't matter how many times you go around as long as you eventually see the sign and follow it.

Demi-Chapter XI:
Dreams

You are never given a wish without also being given the power to make it come true. You may have to work for it, however.

Richard Bach

Keep believing in your special dreams. Do you have a dream, maybe from childhood, that has just stayed around even though life has changed? I love to sing and ever since I saw the *Fabulous Baker Boys*, I have dreamed of being a night club singer with the long sequined dress and the Rosemary Clooney voice – only without the sex, drugs and cigarette smoke. I didn't really want to be a performer, I am really quite shy, but I wanted to sing that sexy, smoky, jazzy love-song way. Now that smoking indoors is illegal and my "give a damn" has loosened considerably, maybe I will do it. Someday.

What dream do you have? From now or way back.   Michelangelo,   THE Michelangelo, is known to have said, "Lord, grant that I may always desire more than I can accomplish."   This is the dude that accomplished more for the art world than almost anyone in 3,000 years of trying, but he dreamed of being a writer. Hey! Me too.

The great part of dreaming is that it does give you something to hope for, something to work for, something to get you up in the morning.   When you have boxed up your dreams (old or new), then in some ways you are living in the moment, but the moment and the meaningfulness in what you are doing is slightly dimmed.

I have been doing a lot of dreaming in the last few years, mostly as a means to figure out what to do when I grow up. Will and I were sitting quietly on a very snowy President's Day when I commented how pleasant it was sitting companionably working together. He said he hadn't done much work yet. I said, quite without thinking, "I'm not doing work-work, I'm doing dream-work." Thinking back on this, I wonder why all work isn't dream work, or why not all of us do what we dream of doing. Why don't we give ourselves permission to do what we want to do without criticism or blame (so long as we are not hurting other people)? Sometimes life gets so big that we forget we even had dreams. Oh, but when they resurface, they are powerful. Do you ever wonder why the "bucket list" is such a popular thing now? I mean the movie was fun, but not really the kind of movie that inspires catch phrases for years to come.

If you have a very special dream, the first step is to admit it to yourself – either say it out loud to yourself or write it down first. Then share it with someone close to you when you are ready. Just saying it out loud is extremely powerful. It doesn't matter if you think that someone else might think the dream is silly, foolish, impossible, etc.- It is your dream and you need to re-examine it. You may decide it is no longer a dream that means that much to you, but that is your choice and only your choice.

Your next step is to figure out exactly what achieving your dream might look like and what is the action plan you need to do to realize your dream; much like keeping promises to yourself. Create a detailed map and timeline just like planning for a journey, which is exactly what you are doing. If you start digging into the work and decide that climbing Everest, while a worthy goal, now seems a little cold for your liking, well, maybe it is more a *fancy* from your youth and not really a dream. If, however, every ounce of your being turns on and starts to buzz when you think about climbing Everest, then maybe that's a dream you need to seriously consider (Or is there a closer, easier, cheaper alternative that might fit the dreamer's bill?). When you believe in yourself and your vision, you are drawing positive energy to you and attracting what you want most.

A friend from church once shared with me that he had a lifelong dream to fly. He is a successful lawyer with a lovely family and sufficient billable hours. A few months earlier he went on a Boy Scout field trip with his son to see a small privately-owned plane. As soon as he sat in the cockpit the buzz came back to him. He had buried it under grown-up responsibility, but the dream had lingered. He started flying lessons and was licensed by the following spring. When he wondered out loud to his wife if he should use the time and money "for something more practical," she said he had been so grumpy before he started his lessons that he had to keep going because it was good for the family. It was a dream he had held onto and had to realize. When we bury, ignore, or just haven't found our passion yet, there is a spark that is just missing until we take the steps to make that dream a reality.

Activity 1.11.1 Dreamscape

(Adapted from "Greatest Pep Talk Ever" in the Oprah Magazine, January 2015). Fill in the blanks on a dream. It may be the same as the promise from Activity 1.8.1 but try to stretch yourself. Write, do, repeat.

STEP 1: CONFRONT YOUR FEARS

1. *If I were truly brave, I would:* (What's the one thing you really want to do?)

2. *But I've been telling myself I can't because:* (List all the reasons you've put off getting started.)

3. *Really, though, the worst thing that could happen is:* (really think of the worst thing)

4. *And if this happened I would:* (How

would you survive it? What would you do?)

5. *Even if the worst happened, I won't give up because*

6. *My bravest friend, _____, would tell me to:* (What sage advice would she/he give you?)

7. *But I'm afraid other people, like _____, (Who are the negatrons?), will say* (What's the worst thing they could come up with?):

_____

8. *If that happens, I will respond by* (plan what you could say or do to boost your confidence):

STEP 2: CALL IN REINFORCEMENTS

Asking for help doesn't make me look weak. When things get hard, I'll call _____ (Who is your greatest supporter?) *because* _____ (How can this person help you reach your goal?) *and* _____ (Who else?)

because _____

(What support does this person give you

when you are working towards a goal?).

Having people "on my team" will help me

feel: _____

STEP 3: DARE YOURSELF TO GET STARTED

I want to begin _____

(What's your goal again?) *right this minute. I*

can _____ (What's your

first move?). *Then, over the next*

_____ (time period) *I can:*

_____.

One of my motivation songs is written

by Garth Brooks and Kent Blazy and

performed by Garth Brooks called, "How

You Ever Gonna Know?" Maybe it will help

you pursue your dream.

[Verse 1]

That old wind that's whipping out there

It's whistling your tune

That wind blew pyramids to Egypt

And footprints to the moon

And that old star that you been wishing on

Is shining mighty bright

But it's the fire inside your heart

That's going to lead you to the light

[Chorus]

How you ever going to know

What it's like to live there

How you ever going to know victory

How you ever going to know

What it's like when dreams become reality

How you ever going to know

How it feels to hold her

How you ever going to know

What it's like to dance

How you ever going to know

If you never take a chance

[Verse 2]

You know failure isn't failure If a
lesson from its learned

I guess love would not be love

Without a risk of being burned

Anything in life worth having

Lord, it has its sacrifice

But the gift that you're receiving

Is worth more than a price

How you ever going to know

What it's like to live there

How you ever going to know

What you never knew

How you ever going to know

If you're down here doing

What the good Lord put you here to do

How you ever going to know

If you could have done it

How you ever going to know

How it feels to fly

How you ever going to know

If you never dare to try Listen not

to the critics

Who put their own dreams on the shelf If you

want to get the truth to admit it

You got to find out for yourself

How you ever going to know

What it's like to be there

How you ever going to know

If you're the best

How you ever going to know

What you believe in

If you don't put it to the test

How you ever going to know

How it feels to hold him

How you ever going to know

What living means

How you ever going to know

If you never chase the dreams

There is something to be said about contentment and being happy with where you are and what you have, but it is okay to have a special dream and you deserve the chance to achieve it. Go you!

Demi-Chapter XII:
Turn Lanes

---

*If you don't change direction, you will
end up where you are heading.*

Lao Tzu

Just turn already. Now that you
know to follow your instincts and you've
picked a dream you just need to have the
nerve to actually do it. One of the most
difficult tasks as a human, or maybe any
living thing, is to be brave regardless of the
opinions of others or the possible outcome.
My father has a way with words. He says
things that have a way of just sticking in our
minds. I know for a fact that all three of us,
his daughters, think of his powerful turns-of
phrase on a regular basis. I am reminded of
the wise words he would say when anyone

was making a decision and considering doing something about it: "Shit or get off the pot." The man is a modern-day Confucius, really.

The point is: do something. One morning on my way to work I was sitting in the left turn lane and had the thoughts that our lives are quite like turn lanes – waiting and then committing to a completely different direction in our lives. Then I quickly found myself on a parallel thought directed at the car in front of me, thinking fondly of my Father's saying and breathing "Just turn already." And this section was born!

So how do we go about making that turn? What is the motivation? If we spend most of our time trying to fix, alter, or cope with a situation, there is a good chance it's not the right one for us. If going straight at the turn fills you with dread, then it isn't the right direction. A lack of choice will make you feel powerless, yet you are the only one behind the wheel in your own life. Staying in one place because you think you have to isn't doing you or your colleagues or partners or loved ones any favors. If you don't want to be there you will not be able to do anything meaningful and very possibly make yourself and others sick or crazy. It is time to take that leap of faith and turn the wheel.

Have I mentioned that I share a birthday with Orville Wright? I also earned my undergraduate degree from Wright State University in Ohio, so I'm a bit of a fan. Charles Kettering, American editor and also a celebrated Ohioan, once said of the Wright Brothers that "they flew right through the smoke screen of impossibility." They turned – probably right. These were two people who were willing to make the decision, take the risk, and experience something marvelous. It doesn't matter if you take the turn at full speed or if you slow to a complete stop beforehand; what matters is that you turn.

When we pull up to the intersections

in our life, we often stall like we are first learning how to drive a manual transmission. Even when we feel lost, bored, frustrated, disengaged or terrified, we continue in the same patterns as before or we freeze, afraid to make any move at all. I learned a really great theory from my therapist prior to my divorce. He helped me understand that when the rational and the emotional match up you are ready to make a decision. Another way to think of it is that when your rational mind starts to consider your emotional health then it is time. Gretchen Rubin writes, in her yearlong *Happiness Project*, that "although we presume that we act because of the way we feel, in fact we often feel because of the way we act." When we don't make the turn, take the chance or change course, we are inviting those feelings of being trapped and afraid to linger. If we make the turn, the future opens up before us. Maybe it is not in that instance and maybe it still takes a bit of driving. If you have turned in the right direction, then the journey is meaningful and satisfying and maybe a little scary, but in a roller-coaster way and not a jumped-out-of-the-plane-without-a-parachute kind of way.

Activity 1.12.1 Turning Radius

Do you have a turn in mind? Think of an area of your life where you want to change directions.

1) State your destination – Describe how you visualize your life once you've made the turn.

2) Plan your approach – which roads do you need to get there?

3) Use your turn signals – who needs to know the change is coming and what the change will be?

4) Watch for oncoming traffic – what financial and emotional impacts do you need to consider?

5) Apply speed. You need just enough

momentum without too much speed – plot out a reasonable timeline for planning and making the turn.

Every major decision takes preparation and thought, just like making a turn. If we attempt to make a 90-degree right hand turn at 55 miles per hour, we may find ourselves upside down and feeling rather battered. However, if we plan our approach, use turn signals (let others know the change is coming), watch for oncoming traffic (consider financial and emotional and physical impacts) and approaches the turn with just enough momentum (nerve), but not too much speed (desperation), then the turn is made safely, smoothly and feels just right.

Demi-Chapter XIII:
Faith

By small and simple things are great things brought to pass.

The Book of Mormon, Alma 37:6

Have faith. Not everyone refers to faith in a religious sense, and that is perfectly fine. There is something much larger than us at work. I am going to use the word faith, but by that I mean your belief in something bigger than the actions you take every day. That may mean a faith in yourself. It may mean a belief in fate or God or karma or serendipity or Batman or the energy of the universe. I am going to use the term faith to encapsulate all of these things and what you might specifically believe.

Taking the right turn requires important preparedness steps, but it also takes a fair amount of faith. You have faith that the drivers of the cars around you share with you a common understanding of the traffic laws, a shared common courtesy, and subscribe to their importance when hurtling down the street in half a ton of powerful fiberglass and steel. You have faith that the 100 billion parts of the vehicle will continue to turn, flap, blow, fire and halt all in perfect order. You have faith in the thermodynamics that make the firmness of the asphalt something you never even have to think about. Maybe that doesn't actually apply in places where the temps reach 120 degrees in the summer, but then, no one goes outside there anyway. You have faith that you can stay coordinated enough and strong enough to turn the wheel (without spilling your latte, sending your dog caroming off your lap or pulling a muscle). You also have faith that it is exactly what you need to be doing.

Everyday living takes an enormous amount of faith itself. When everyday life gets hairy, it takes an even sturdier faith to get through. Following my divorce, I was in a deep well of doubt and hurt. I hadn't practiced any kind of faith for almost ten years. One night, in the depth of my deepest sadness, while lying on my bedroom floor, I decided that I needed a bible. I got up, got dressed and went to the bookstore. I bought the first bible that wasn't the picture version. This bible was written by T.D. Jakes just for women and had very special sections just to help women see themselves in the stories of the bible. That bible began the spark that rekindled my faith in myself and God, which was what I needed at the time. As my journey continued and I found a church to believe in. I found my footing in faith growing stronger. Over the next few years, I raged against the dissonance in my heart: my need to control my life and my complete inability to control any aspect of my life. When Will and I struggled with our relationship, I learned to turn my life over to the plan my God has for me. I do my best every day. I pray, I reflect, I make the best choices I can, and I rely on faith for the rest. I have to believe in the goodness of humanity, the rationality of physics, the predictability of human behavior and the power of gratitude. Even now, when I feel myself overwhelmed with doubt – in the plan, in what to do next, in myself – I reach deep inside to my little bud of faith.

There are others I know who have such a deep abiding faith that I am inspired and overwhelmed by their ability to know that whatever happens is for best, even if that appears to be monumentally unfortunate. I am a church marque inspiration junky. I'll admit it. I'm in a program for it. I cannot help craning my neck to see what clever and inspirational message is on any church's message board when I drive past. Sometimes it is just an announcement of service times but sometimes, oh boy, sometimes, it is a gem! I love this one, on the Christ Community Church message board in Denver: "Hope is faith holding its hand out in the dark." Hallelujah, Brother. I liked it so much I drove around the block and parked and got out of my car to take a picture of it. This small phrase has helped me through some dark times indeed. May it help you in your dark days. Amen.

This is not a 21st century struggle. Julian of Norwich lived to the ripe old age of seventy-four in the late 14th century. That, in itself, is a minor miracle. Julian served the English as an anchoress and respected spiritual counselor. Her work, *Revelations of Divine Love,* is the first book in the English language known to have been written by a woman. Julian is known to have assured her readers and devotees that the best way to deal with misery and travails is to believe completely in God's love. She reminds us to allow ourselves to trust in the world larger than our own, "And all shall be well, and All manner of things shall be well." A friend gave this to me when I first moved to Colorado and I call on it to remind me to stop and breathe and let it be.

Is faith something we can nurture? Can we build our faith? Faith is a principle that must be coupled with action. If we are not willing to act, then we do not have faith. Have you ever attended one of those teambuilding activity courses? There is an activity where you are asked to trust (have faith in) your teammates to catch you as you fall back, blindly, into their arms. You have faith that they will not be distracted by a hangnail, an Elvis impersonator or the desire to watch you crash to the ground. You have that faith, but it is not real until you lean back and fall. Once they catch you and you are safe and smiling, your faith is increased. With each opportunity to have our faith tested our faith is strengthened, and we are more willing to believe and act the next time. 18th Century English writer, Samuel Johnson is famous for his quotation of a Spanish proverb that says, "'He who would bring home the wealth of the Indies, must carry the wealth of the Indies with him.' So, it is in travelling; a man must carry knowledge with him, if he would bring home knowledge." Similarly, she must carry faith with her if she hopes to increase her faith.

Activity 1.13.1 Read & Reflect

"Life has meaning only in the struggle. Triumph or defeat is in the hands of the Gods. So, let us celebrate the struggle!"

- Stevie Wonder

Think about a struggle in your life that resulted in a blessing. Concentrate on the lessons learned, the positive outcome and the blessing that came from the pain or difficultly. Return to this reflection during any challenging time in your life and remember that we are not given anything in this life that we are not given the tools to overcome. It is through faith that we accomplish all things.

One of my favorite phrases is often attributed to the bible but is not, in actuality, in the bible at all. "God never said life would be easy, He just promised it would be worth it." Even if God didn't say that, I still like it. Some smarty-pants did say it and it is right. Most of the hardest things we do in our lives turn out to be very, very worth it. Childbirth is a terrible struggle for both mother and child, but both would agree that it is worth it. I recently finished a singlehanded master-suite remodel that it took me over six months. It was incredibly hard work, my hands did not thank me, my back did not thank me, but my imagination, my creative passion, my HGTV addiction – they all thanked me. I never doubted for a minute that I could do it. I had faith that I could do it. I astonished myself with how well I did it.

With each phase of the project my faith in myself grew. I remodeled five rooms and a hallway. I designed, painted, tiled, installed cabinets, and found the final touches to make it the perfect master suite for me. When we focus on what we think we cannot do, our past difficulties and fears, we struggle to nurture positive feelings about the next step and the chapter. But life sends us little serendipities, little victories, and little miracles to assure us we can do it. I wrote this first book in about three months, working part time. When I finished the first draft on the last day of 2015, I couldn't stop smiling. I had faith that I could do it, I had faith that I should do it and now I have faith that people will want to read it. Thank you, by the way, for your faith that the last six chapters will be as helpful as the first fourteen.

Demi-Chapter XIV:
Thigh Master

Created by abyley

Love your body. I hate to say it, but this is another obvious and almost impossible tip. This isn't just for women – men feel just as much pressure to conform to the physical archetype. Many of us have struggled all of our lives with our body image, our weight, our physical health, our fitness levels. While this goes hand in hand with taking good care of yourself, there is something more to it. Loving your body is a vital step to loving yourself, as you are, with all you have to offer.

Unfortunately, this isn't as easy as reading a few pages of "go you" propaganda. This is deep, inside, work. This is constantly reaffirming the blessings of your body until you convince yourself and rewire your thinking. And even then, it is a fragile, delicate, crystal structure that can be shaken and shattered with one external tremor.

Let's think about what we can do to build this internal scaffold of strength and confidence and what we can use to help us keep it strong. We start with an attitude of gratitude, so to speak. What do you think when you look at yourself in the mirror? If you are like me, you probably zero in on the specific areas that you dislike or are disappointed with the most. Do you look in the mirror and think something like this: "Sigh… my tummy is poochy today"? I shouldn't have eaten that pizza. If I could stand up straight, it might look better. I really need to get rid of these inches right here" (generally accompanied by squeezing, pinching, holding in or flattening).   I'd be lying if I said I didn't do this or if I said that a single one of my friends hasn't done this at some point in his or her life.   I'm pretty sure my dog, Echo, sucks in her tummy when she walks past the full-length mirror.   Even the most beautiful women have these moments.

The point isn't to never have them, but to keep them short and fend them off quickly, before any damage is done.   Tyra Banks, the super-model, started out considering herself an ugly duckling, being rejected by a handful of modeling agencies before starting her modeling career at age fifteen.   Even the beautiful Ms. Banks had to work through self-doubt and self-criticism.   She gives all of us, super model or not, this advice: "Stop saying these negative things about yourself. Look in the mirror and find something about yourself that's positive and celebrate that!"   Try Tyra's advice in

Activity 1.14.1 Mirror, Mirror

Using Tyra Banks' advice, go stand in front of a mirror. Now is the time to force yourself to think differently. Copy this activity and hang it on the mirror. Ideally, you will want to be able to do this activity naked. You may not be there at first and that is totally okay. As you get better at this, try to do it closer and closer to your naked-as-you-were-born state. Once you can do this confidently, with a smile, and truly believe what you are saying, then your internal structure is built, and your work will be to keep it strong.

As you look in the mirror identify three positive attributes* about your physical self. Don't hear the negative voices. Don't compare yourself to anyone else. What is there to love about YOUR BODY?

1. _____

2. _____

3. _____

Repeat at least once a week. Add more to the original three as often as you can.

* Some of us start this activity from a place so low that we cannot find a single positive attribute yet. If you feel this is you, then just stand in front of the mirror and look. Focus on not hearing the negatives. Just look. Don't state any opinions. Start with 1 minute and work up to the activity above.

Some of you may remember when Oprah, another one of us who struggled with her self-image for decades, spent an entire year, with all of us watching, losing so much weight she had to drag the equivalent in pig fat onto the stage in a Radio Flyer wagon. She looked and felt marvelous, but, boy, the struggle! She has, as is inevitable for some of us who try to fight our natural bodies, put some of that weight back on. But now, she is marvelous and confident and more self-assured at sixty than ever. Even

Oprah, the millionaire media mogul with a heart of gold, worried about her body image. She does a similar exercise as the activity you just did (1.14.1). In her May 2014 she stands in front of the mirror and blesses her body from head to foot. I do a blessing like this each morning in my morning prayers before I get out of bed. Sometimes it sticks for the day, sometimes it doesn't, but I feel it is the least I can do for having forty mostly pain-free years (and the pain I have had has been almost entirely self-inflicted by my own unhealthy habits).

How do we start to feel good in our own skin? I did not really understand that phrase until a few years ago when I really started to feel uncomfortable in my skin. It was a little of the body image stuff. I did not see that for years, however. My first reaction? Try a diet. Go gluten free. Do the blood-type diet (both of which I do think are healthy options for me but did not fix the problem). Then I tried body wraps to squeeze all the cellulite out of my fat cells, then I tried weird detoxes. Then I went back to soda and cheese and made an appointment to see my doctor.

Weight loss is my go-to problem. I default to the thought that if I can fix my body, I can fix my life. When something is uneasy in my life, I feel that my skin is too tight, that I am wearing the suit of some size-2 girl. For some reason I feel like I can control my body issues when other aspects of my life are out of control. The truth is – I really cannot. When I fail at a diet or blow my exercise regimen then I feel like failure in this area too – something I should be able to control. Now I feel terrible about all the other crap AND my body image. I then feel even worse about myself. I am slowly moving towards accepting my body for what it is and that it is pretty awesome as it is. That is something I can control – how I feel about my body. And you can too.

That is absolutely marvelous, and I am

all inspired by myself and my great attitude. But HOW? This question often reminds me of one of my college mathematics professors who would skip 130 steps in a complex mathematical proof by saying they were intuitively obvious. Truly accepting who we are needs a little more direct instruction.

Here are four intuitively obvious steps to get you started. Step one: Praise Yourself. Any time we have a thought or hear an opinion from others, our brain builds a neural pathway. Whether that thought be positive or negative, it becomes a connection in our brain. I think of it as a path in an overgrown field. If you only walk that way once, the grass springs back up. If you walk that way, and then your cousin follows, and then a heard of deer meander along it and then the neighbor kids start riding their bikes on it, that path becomes so well worn it may never grow back. The healthy grass is dead while that path is being used. When we start making new paths, we are giving the worn one time to grow over and disappear again. For example, instead of looking in the mirror and sighing angrily about your armpit cleavage while pulling on a cardigan over your tank top, stop at that thought and find one thing about yourself that looks good today. Focus on your shoes, your hair, the fact that your partner loves you, that your cat has never once (to your face) insulted your outfit. If you walk this path every day instead, the armpit-fat path will grow over, and you'll stop believing it and maybe even stop seeing it.

Step two: Don't believe what they say. When I was born at seven pounds eight ounces, my Grandmother dubbed me "Butterball" – either in honor of the Turkey or the Christmas cookie – no one is quite sure on that point. I've decided she must have meant the round, pale, nutty and sweet butterball cookie. This should have been a charming and affectionate nickname, but like most nicknames, it did not have the charming and affirming effect on the receiver. I can't blame my Grandmother and her old-world Croatian "I calls it as I sees it" nature. I am quite sure it was meant both as a charming compliment and as a subtle hint to my mother that I would run to fat. Had I been more than six months old and more precocious and self-confident when she died I would have called her Grandma Schnoz-of-the-Sauerkraut-House and we would have laughed about it. Unfortunately, it has not worked out that way and the label "Butterball" has stayed with me all of my life.

At some point, around twenty-five, I started exercising, eating better and lost most of that baby-weight, about fifty pounds of it. About twice a year now, the Butterball name floats back across my mind. I joke about it, or use it to relate to others that I was a rather portly child, but even then, and even now when writing this, I can still feel my chest constrict. It's like being bullied by my own mind and my own kin from beyond the grave. I am letting this neural pathway grow over a little more every year. Someday, I will never use that path and may even forget it was ever there. It is my choice to choose a different path.

Step three: Be realistic. Over the past fifteen years about fifteen of those pounds have returned, but, like Oprah, I am trying to accept my body as it wants to be. My doctor, while exploring reasons for my various symptoms, told me that "it might just be that your body likes to be around 150 pounds." I keep thinking about that. There is not one person whose body perfectly matches any chart you'll see in a magazine or doctor's office. Those are all averages. Your body, regardless of how hard you work, might just like to be at a certain weight. Not that I couldn't be a healthier 150 pounds. I certainly could and that is what I am focusing on now. Berating my body and having anything but gratitude for all it does every day is just pointless. Martha Beck once tackled the question that strikes fear in the heart of any man. Even Ironman would flinch. "Do I Look Fat in This?" In her powerful truth-telling way, she got right to the point. "Some clothes make you look slightly larger, some slightly smaller, but here's the truth: Whatever you're wearing, you look approximately as fat as you are. Accepting that fact frees up a ton of energy, lightening you considerably." I think that is a perfect statement and I hate that it is completely true.

The fact that it is completely true is what started the shapewear craze in the 16th Century. Corset, anyone? The cartoon character Maxine once stated that if George Washington never told a lie, clearly Martha Washington never asked if her corset made her look fat. And, yes, men often wore shapeware then too – and hose! Who says we are more liberated now? Every century has had its form of squeezy, slimming or bolstering devices to allow us to pretend we look slightly more or less than we are. I completely banished the padded bra from my lingerie drawer in my twenties. Why fake it? If that person you are trying to impress ever gets under the padding, he/she will know the truth anyway. And, seriously, there are now panties you can wear to make your butt look *bigger*? I

> That's the real secret to dressing well: It's all about attitude.... It's about walking into a room, knowing that you look and feel good, and projecting that attitude out to everyone who sees you. – Betty Halbreich, *Secrets of a Fashion Therapist*

can't imagine, having myself a rearview that Julia Sugarbaker, from the T.V. show *Designing Women*, would refer to as "an ass you can serve tea off of." That's right – I was born with a built-in bustle and pannier – just two centuries too late. But I am realistic about that. Now, I just work on the consistency – more brie and less cottage cheese.

Step four: Take charge. What should we do to change our mindsets, then? We are the leaders of our own lives and we can believe what we want to believe about ourselves. We can decide whether the label is true or not. We can also embrace this reality – either do something about it or stop criticizing yourself. Either you are deciding to accept who you are. Sometimes we just have to accept the struggles – the migraines, disabilities, food allergies, pain – and find a way to learn from the pain. Focusing on the positives are the best way to overcome the pain.

Helen Mirren is a gorgeous, smart, confident woman at 68 years old. I want to be like that. Her husband of decades told an AARP reporter:

> "It's a function of mindset.... Helen has an innate sense of who she is, and a confidence and directness.... What's sexy is how she is in the world even more than how she looks, though she certainly looks beautiful."

Feeling beautiful has nothing to do with

how other people see you. You can feel beautiful (or handsome) in grungy clothes or your best evening wear. Figure out what makes you feel healthy and beautiful and do that, be with that person, wear that thing, eat that food. You define your own perception of yourself as healthy, fit, beautiful, and happy with who you are.

Activity 1.14.2 Channeling Your Confidence Role Model

Reading this again makes me think of the popular catchphrase, fake it until you make it. Not that Dame Helen is faking it, but you and I are trying to get ourselves there with positive thoughts and confidence.

When you walk into a room, think about how Helen Mirren would walk into a room.

She's not the queen (though she's played one on TV), she's real and confident.

Choose someone you feel is a role

model for you for confidence and positive body image. It doesn't have to be Helen, J. Lo, Oprah or anyone famous. It can be a friend, a relative or someone at work.

Truthfully, you don't even have to know her or him. What you must know is that they show themselves in a way that you want to emulate to the world. Deep down, they are all struggling or did struggle with what we are working on today, but they present themselves to the world with confidence. I don't want you to be disingenuous, fake or inauthentic. I want you to find and love the real you that is hiding inside by emulating the behaviors of someone who speaks to you. That's our goal for this activity.

1) Body Image Role Model (name):

_____

2) What does she/he do that you admire and want to emulate for yourself (be as specific as you can about the actions or behaviors):

_____

3) What will you do to emulate these behaviors:

_____

Once you have tried this emulation, describe how doing so made you feel.

_____

Our one last thought about this topic comes from the song, "Hate Yourself," written by Hillary Lindsey and Brett James and performed by Kellie Pickler:

Verse 2:

Every cover of every magazine

Makes you feel like you're not thin enough

Not pretty enough

You let a stupid pair of old blue jeans

That don't quite fit ruin your day

And you beat yourself up

You beat yourself up

But blue jeans ain't nothin'

But fabric and buttons

They don't mean a thing

They can't make you beautiful

Baby, you're beautiful So throw 'em away

[Chorus:]
Cause life's too short
To hate yourself
To try to be someone else
So, quit wasting your time
The days go by way too fast
To let anything hold you back
So, don't cry anymore Cause life's too short To
hate yourself.

Demi-Chapter XV:
The Gift of Cheese

While we are living in the present, we must celebrate life every day, knowing that we are becoming history with every work, every action, every deed.
Mattie Stepanek

Honor your accomplishments. Recall the last time you congratulated yourself for a job well done. If it was earlier today, then you can probably skip this section for now. If you cannot remember the last time you recognized something wonderful that you did, then I'm going to ask you to think a bit harder. In Demi-Chapter one you pronounced what you made lovely. This is close to what we are talking about in this section – a step in the right direction. This section is about celebrating your life and rewarding yourself for all the big and little accomplishments in every day.

Cheese is a powerful reward for me. If I had been alive during the depression, my sign would have said "Will work for cheese."

The American philosophy of reward is interesting. We work very, very hard, in general, yet we often feel terribly guilty for being recognized or touting our own success. However, if we are not recognized we feel resentful and if we taut our own talents we are lacking humility. We do tend to get ourselves into quite a celebratory pickle. How do we recognize our blessings, our talents, the good parts of our life without feeling like unworthy braggarts?

Celebrating doesn't have to mean extravagance (though it certainly can). Celebrating can be as simple as a quiet cup of tea and a square of chocolate or a rowdy beer with friends. Celebrating can be lifting your Coke Zero in a toast to your partner, who just finished a difficult and complicated task at work. Celebrating can mean, recognizing that you have exercised every day this week and tonight you are freeing yourself from the pressure of having to complete a seventh workout. Celebrating can be just giving yourself permission to smile and take a deep breath of satisfaction. Celebrating may be allowing yourself time and solitude. For some, this daily celebration might be a glass of wine, an hour in the bathtub, a game of Call of Duty Zombies or a guilt free evening of searching travel sites for the next big trip.

What does this have to do with cheese, you may be asking. A friend who read the manuscript before this section was written thought it would be about change – as in *Who Moved My Cheese?* – but it is actually about how you reward yourself and what pleasures you find in your life. For me, I choose cheese. And Garth Brooks (the songs, not the man himself though I am sure he is a lovely chap). Echo also chooses cheese. A day without cheese in our home is like a day without sunshine.

A small bit of cheese each morning, like a small bit of chocolate each night, is my reward for a day well-lived. There is a reason most of us remember the sultry voice saying, "Behold the Power of Cheese" on those commercials many years ago. For me, cheese has the power of the daily celebration.

Many of us, however, don't give ourselves daily celebrations. We give ourselves more on our to-do list. We give ourselves the head shake of disappointment because we only did twenty minutes of yoga instead of the full hour. We rarely allow ourselves to see what we did accomplish today and celebrate that. So, in this section, I am going to ask you to celebrate all that you have done and all that you have to celebrate in your life.

I also love to sing. A terribly sad day arrived about six years ago. I stopped singing in the shower. I thought that this was because of a three-week bout with bronchitis, but upon reflection, I think it was because I had lost my song. I even stopped … GASP … car-singing! As I work to find my joy again, I can feel my song coming back. Singing is like the fat-free version of cheese. Andrea Bocelli, one of the world's most famous Italian-born tenors, speaks of singing as: "we sing, and we celebrate the beauty that we can grow and live every day." Through my singing, I am communicating that I feel empowered, that I feel hope, that I am proud of who I am and what I can do. We all have our own way of celebrating and to do it every day, you must find your daily celebration.

Let's identify your daily celebration. Do you pause each evening and name the things you did well today? I'd ask why not, but we all know that it is because we aren't "supposed to." Charlize Theron, during an interview following her Academy Award, stated: "I think today women are very scared to celebrate themselves, because then they just get labeled." If this is a fear for you, let's just start small. My cheese, chocolate and singing celebrations are all done privately (unless my car windows are open).

This isn't out of a fear to be labeled as much a preference towards shyness and I spend the vast majority of my non-work time by myself.

How we celebrate our small wins each day is a very personal choice, often a very difficult and guilt-ridden choice. It is easier for us to plan a big hullabaloo for a big accomplishment than to honor our daily achievements. I think we should do both! By honoring each day, you, as Magic Johnson advises, "celebrate the life you [have], not the life you could've had."

Activity 1.15.1 Finding Your Reason to Celebrate

"Lord knows, every day is not a success,
every year is not a success. You have to
celebrate the good."
- Reese Witherspoon

List five things that you did well today. These can be as simple as got to work on time or as complicated as saved a child from taking her own life. Now explain to yourself why each of these things is important, impactful and worth celebrating.

Once you have held your daily celebrations, honoring your achievements, every day for a few weeks, it will become a natural part of your day. I think you will also find that how you see yourself in every part of your day will also change. You will be kinder to yourself and more willing to see the good in your life every day. Once you learn to celebrate you – be it with cheese, song or walk with the dog – you'll find there is more in life to celebrate.

Activity 1.15.2 Party for One

Now that you have five things to celebrate about today, how will you toast yourself?

Step one: List the first five rewarding pleasures that come to your mind.

Step two: Look at each pleasure and determine if each one is a "big" reward or a "daily" regard. Label each reward as a daily, weekly, monthly, yearly, or lifetime reward. Keep repeating steps one and two until you have found three to five ways you can celebrate your daily successes. Try to think about daily rewards that you can afford in both time and money. I will encourage you to make time for your daily celebrations, but you also have to be realistic. A 90-minute massage might be the best reward imaginable for you, but it may be too costly and time consuming as a daily reward.

Step three: Make time. Once you have identified a handful of small daily celebration options, figure out how and when you can have your little party for one. Just like any new habit, you will have to make the time and work at keeping the time open.

It is often difficult to allow ourselves a reward for a life well-lived. Or even for a day well-done. You can take it too far, but you must take it. You deserve it and you have worked hard each day to earn it. Don't be afraid to acknowledge all the good you have done in this world.

Demi-Chapter XVI: Inspiration

Let yourself be inspired. Inspiration. Why is it so damn scary and why do we usually just ignore it? There is a strange belief out there in the world that inspiration is fleeting or doesn't exist at all and if you do sense something that is inspiring, it is probably just gas, mental instability, selfishness or too much of a risk to pay attention to. Inspiration is the thing that makes you smile, that drives you forward, that makes what you are doing feel worthwhile, or that makes your heart grow three sizes in one day. Yet it can also prompt us to do things differently, do things that are scary, give up some security or buck the system. Luckily, we do all those things with a smile, so it almost always evens out in the end.

Sometimes we are inspired for a moment (like the moment at the Grand Canyon when the clouds part, the sun shines, the fog lifts, and the heavenly hosts sing "Hallelujah! Get out your cameras"), sometimes for an hour ("I think I will write that letter to Dorothy") and sometimes for years ("the work I do each day is meaningful and prompts me to be excited about it"). Inspiration looks and feels differently to each of us. It is our job to notice it. I have a friend who relates inspiration to a mega caffeine rush. She says that when she gets that burst of energy, all of her senses tingle and she can't stop smiling or talking at 220 words-per-minute. For me, I get a similar, though admittedly more low-key, feeling. My muscles coil up tight, like I am about to spring. I also feel this big warm glow inside, like my heart is growing three sizes. It feels like it is too big to fit inside my body. Generally, I must get up and do something about the idea that second or the light will go out and I will lose it.

The inspiration for this book came after a very stressful, but successful year of work. I was on a solo road trip through Moab, Arches and the Canyonlands National Parks in Utah. I was seeking quiet, calm and the time to just let my heart stop racing. I had driven onto a small side road above the Canyonlands. I saw a dirt turn off and drove down that until I came to the canyon. I found this marvelous and perfectly quiet location on the canyon edge. I sat. I took pictures. I journaled. It was when I was snacking on a small chocolate that I was inspired. (Is chocolate the secret to inspiration?) It was at that moment that I knew I wanted to write a book. I wanted to be heard. I wanted to share all that I have learned with others. Maybe I could theme it after the sayings in the candy wrappers

(Ultimately, that didn't work out and I am so glad it didn't!) and maybe it would help to inspire others. Energy swelled up in me like I had only felt a few times before – the clarity of mind that comes with a problem-solved or a path unearthed. I almost felt like I was aglow. I could count the times I felt and followed that feeling on both hands, but all of them led to successful and meaningful actions. Like faith, the more you acknowledge and act on your inspirations, the more they come. I immediately began to make notes. I jotted ideas, structures, and themes. The inspiration flowed out of me. If I hadn't done that immediately, then there is a good chance that the ideas would have been lost. Or at least buried for another decade. In truth, I have never looked back at the journal entry. I have never had to. By writing it all down, I forever stamped it into my mind and even though I've spent the subsequent years until now making little steps, the inspiration changed my entire life because I identified it and responded to it.

How does inspiration feel for you?

Author Michael Nolan tells us that 'there are many things in life that will catch your eye, but only a few will catch your heart... pursue those things." Activity 1.16.1 will help you to identify the feeling of inspiration so that you can embrace it the next time it occurs.

Activity 1.16.1 Inspiration Feels Like...

1) *Think of a time when you both felt inspired and followed that inspiration.* I am asking you for both, because the feeling will be easier for you to identify. If you have never followed the inspiration, do your best to remember the feeling. If you do not believe you have ever been inspired, try to identify the feelings of a time when you truly enjoyed what you were doing at the time and lost yourself in the moment.

2) *Describe what you were doing when the inspiration came.* Had you been specifically looking for it or did it come "out of

the blue"? Be as descriptive as you can –
describe the time, place, what you were doing
and your frame of mind in as much detail as
possible. Try to put yourself back into that
moment.

3) *Now, focus in on the physical
feeling. What did your body do when you hit the
inspiration point? Describe the feeling.*

4) *How did you respond? What did
you do immediately upon feeling the
inspiration?*

5) *What was the result of
responding or not responding to the
inspiration?*

Can we actively seek inspiration, or does
doing so make it artificial? I say we can seek it
out or at least be open to it when it chooses to
come. One important way to be open to it is to
quiet the daily noise that hides from us the
whirring and purring of our minds. David
Hendy, author of *Noise: A Human History*,

suggests that we get away from traffic noise. This, he continues, among all of modern society's noises, is most disruptive to finding inspiration. Have you ever been in a hotel room next to a crying baby? A bachelor party? A high school marching band trip? This is noise that you cannot control, and it can be much more disruptive than the noise you are familiar with and can control at home like the furnace turning on or your spouse's snoring (though that can sometimes be categorized with the rumble of a MAC engine). Hendy suggests seeking out places without car and truck noises, but with the general hum of human life. I would suggest that this is a great way to start if you are unaccustomed to quiet. Jumping headfirst into silence can be shocking. The saying that silence is deafening is quite true. If you are not ready for the shock of silence, I would definitely suggest that you ease into it by slowly eliminating the sounds of humanity – start with traffic, then maybe it is the clicking of the clock, which will be alarmingly loud to you, then maybe comes the dog's breathing, the scratching of the mice in the walls, the sound of water through the water heater. As you eliminate noise, your senses tune in to sounds you did not even know were happening. While I was sitting on the edge of the canyon, watching the wind, I was suddenly startled by the roar of a jet plane overhead, incredibly close overhead. I looked about frantically to see the white trail of jet stream in the sky, but nothing was there. As it roared past me again, and I jumped again at the surprising loudness, I realized that this was not a fighter plane at all, but simply the sound of a passing sparrow as it dove and wheeled on the air currents around the canyon, absent of car noises, cell phones, mechanical whirring and ticking clocks. It was a sound I had never noticed before and will never forget. Like inspiration, once you hear it, you cannot unhear it. Once you start paying attention, it becomes harder and harder to ignore.

At any point in this process you may find yourself hearing your inner voice telling you that inspiration is at hand. Inspiration can happen anywhere once you are ready to receive it. Stoplights, showers, and boring meetings when you are watching out of the windows and thinking about sandwiches, can be some of the most common occurrences for inspiration. There's a legend that a famous Austrian composer once wrote his masterpiece after inspiration came to him while eating a cheese sandwich. Perhaps sandwiches are the key to inspiration. I do love a good sandwich. But then, it did contain cheese. Cheese – not just for celebrating anymore? Or perhaps the key is that inspiration comes when we let go and allow it to come. When our mind is distracted by the yummy or shiny, it is more open to letting inspiration sneak in rather when watching obsessively for it to arrive. Like the good old saying a watched pot doesn't boil, demanded inspiration will stubbornly refuse to arrive. Like happiness, the more we seek it the harder it is to find. When we clear our mind of the noise, there is more room for inspiration to visit and hang out for a while. We can even invite inspiration in. Inspiration, like faith, energy, our instincts and any other skills we wish to sharpen, comes with practice and an invitation to stick around for a while. Picasso is known to have once said in response to how he found his inspiration for his work that "inspiration exists, but it must find you working." Note to self: once you send the invitation, it is best to get to work and not just sit on the couch eating bonbons and waiting for it to arrive.

The next activity will help you to invite inspiration into your heart and mind. You will need to identify your favorite solo activity and when and where you will be able to have time to do this favorite solo activity in a quiet place.

Activity 1.16.2 Invite inspiration in

1)   Identify   your   favorite   solo

activity that disconnects you from the hecticness of life. Running, baking, quilting, playing Call of Duty, all qualify if they bring you peace of mind. If it is too mentally active, though, you may not be making enough room for inspiration to come.

2)   Locate a time and place where you can have quiet. If you live in the city and you run in the afternoon, maybe you need to leave the city to find quiet. If you bake, you may need to get up before the rest of the family to enjoy the silence of the sleeping house. Think creatively about how you will find a quiet place. This doesn't necessarily mean deathly silent; it means quieter than your usual space.

3)   Give yourself at least an hour of silent time to do your favorite activity. Be sure to have a way to record inspiration – notebook, phone app, voice memo, etc.

4)   Before you begin, say out loud an area of your life where you need inspiration or a problem you are trying to solve.

5) That's it. Now engage fully in your activity. Let your mind go. Do not think on the area or the problem. Dive into the activity and let it fill your mind. Depending on how practiced you are at inspiration-harvesting, you may find that it takes longer or more sessions.

6) When a thought comes to your mind about the problem, check how your body reacts. If you do not feel the physical response that you described in activity 1.16.1, then ignore the thought and focus on your activity. If you do feel that feeling in your body, stop the activity and do something about the inspiration – write, give yourself a voice memo, phone a friend – do anything you can to not forget the inspiration.

7) Repeat this activity as needed until #6 happens or until you run out of the need for inspiration in your life. Which, by the way, doesn't happen.

Remember that the only way to

guarantee inspiration in your life is to recognize and act on the inspiration that you receive. Once you learn to recognize the physical and emotional responses to an inspiration, you receive more and more. If you stop receiving inspiration, which will happen due to burnout, stress, distraction, or just too much mental noise, repeat the activities in this section until you are in-tune once more.

Demi-Chapter XVII:
Your Path

Do or do not. There is no try.

-Yoda

Find your path. Know your path.
People start asking us what we want to be when we grow up at – what? – four years old? When we say, fireman, magician, teller of stories, professional jockey, or snowman, they tussle our hair and tell us how cute or smart we are in a way that clearly communicates (if our four-year-old minds were ready for context clues) that there is no way we will possibly be those things, but aren't we adorable for thinking we might.

And here many of us are, decades later, still wanting to be something we felt prompted to do when we were younger but did not do for lots of reasons. Maybe what you did for decades was the perfect thing, but now it is not. That might be one of the worst feelings – I thought this was 'my calling' and now it isn't. Our lives are long and full. I used to think that having one path on which I trod faithfully and from which I never parted was the right way to lead my life. It showed loyalty and stick-to-itiveness. If one was truly successful, one found a (single) career and shined like a super star until it ended with a crystal apple and one-hundred thirty-seven thousand binder clips holding your life's work together.

There are shelves and shelves of books out there that focus solely on this topic – what am I supposed to do with my life? Jen Hatmaker, writer and mother (hilarious, by the way – a must read), suggests that, me, writing this, and you, reading it, get to struggle over this question because "we are educated and financially stable." This is absolutely true. And it's also absolutely not true. The guilt is a first world, middle-class and above, luxury, but wanting a meaningful life is everyone's right. Some of us "fret over the perception of wasting our lives" because "the worry of putting food on the table isn't a daily, crushing worry." But having a meaningful life is also a human dream, perhaps a human right, to be able to do what you love and love what you do every day. We all still want to have meaningful lives, regardless of our socio-economic status.

I struggle with the guilt of this question. Right now, it is a Thursday afternoon and I am sitting in a sun-filled home office, in a safe and secure country, happily writing these words and munching on crackers (gluten free and organic, of course). I would not be able to do this without the blessings of my life that allow it. Most of us struggle with the guilt that accompanies this question. I have stayed in my education job and am blessed with a great salary and benefits package, a fairly flexible schedule, a wonderfully empathetic supervisor and I work with some of the kindest and smartest humans on the planet. And yet, here I am, asking the question. Is there more I should be doing with my life? Is it fair? Do I have a right to love the work I am asked to do every day? It seems like entitlement; and entitlement makes me both indignant (when it appears in others) and sheepishly guilty (when it appears in me). My friend Eileen refers to this as the golden handcuffs. Some of you may feel locked into your life right now, too. Let's unlock our lives together, shall we? I'll write, and you read. It'll be a-w-e-s-o-m-e! Smiley face thumbs up.

Here's a thought. We have a right to be happy and, since we do not have to worry about survival, generally, we have a responsibility to utilize our status and our talents to make the world a better place. Elizabeth Gilbert, author of *Eat, Pray, Love*, told Katie Arnold-Ratliff, in a *2013* interview that she believes a talent that is not used "metastasizes and becomes a burden." I believe that this applies to more than just talent, it also applies to passion. For me, my life goal is to leave this place better than I found it. Am I perfect? Oh, good grief, no. You know that from the first one-hundred forty pages. I do believe that I have made a difference in the lives of hundreds of people – small and momentary, in some cases, hopefully larger in others. I do feel I will leave this life better than when I arrived in it. I also am discovering that I believe it is our responsibility to live our best lives in order to leave this world a better place. Part of that involves finding your path. Maryanne Radmacher, author and artist, advises us to "live with intention: do what

 you love."

      *Language disclaimer: We are going to use the word path to mean destiny, personal calling, Personal Legend, plan, meaning and all other similarly inspiring words. You may call it whatever resonates with you. Feel free to scribble out path and write your own word in as needed.

I am going to spend a fair bit of time in this section with Paulo Coelho, author of *The Alchemist*. Coelho's main character is advised that "to realize one's destiny is a person's only obligation… And when you want something, all the universe conspires in helping you to achieve it." I believe our path is more than just something we want. Our path is a necessary part of how we are meant to spend our life on this earth.

Do some of us miss our path? Yes. And some wander back and forth, on and off, over their years. Some find their path when young and have the joy of staying on it all of their lives. Sir Ken Robinson, author of *The Element* and TED Talk Megastar, guides us to "never underestimate the vital importance of finding early in life the work that for you is play." That said, we are also never too old to find the work that carries the meaning and purpose that makes a hard day's work feel wonderful. That is our task for today.

Why is finding this path so important to our lives? There are some of you, my dear readers, who are either staunchly on your paths or are not yet at a point where you feel the need to think about your path. Bless your sweet little hearts and feel free to move on and come back when you need to. For the rest of us, the sense of emptiness that comes from leaving, changing, or not yet finding, our paths can lead to much despair, unease and unhappiness. At some point, I believe, we each must find our path to truly feel whole and centered and to make this world better than it was the day our precious little heinies entered it. Robinson also tells us, from his research, that without finding and connecting with your true talents, which lead to your true path, you can never know what you are truly capable of achieving and whose life you are capable of touching.

Robinson references Aleksandr Solzhenitsyn's statement "I believe if we begin with ourselves and do the things that we need to do and become the best person we can be; we have a much better chance of changing the world for the better." Amen, brother.

Our paths are not necessarily clear cut and constant all of our lives. That does not mean that we have left the path. We wouldn't learn much in this life if our path never meandered, but we should have a sense of what our path is. I am going to ask you to think historically about your path in the activity that follows.

Activity 1.17.1 Historical Pathfinding

You are going to reconstruct your path over your life. Below is an empty box in which you can draw anything that represents your path so far. You can choose how you want to represent your path visually, including Love/Relationships, Health, or Career or some other important areas of your life. Describe your life path in each of these areas, dividing your life into as many segments as needed to correspond to your years here on earth or the bends in your path. A simple version of my path for career is on the next page as an example. Notice the turning points that impacted my career.

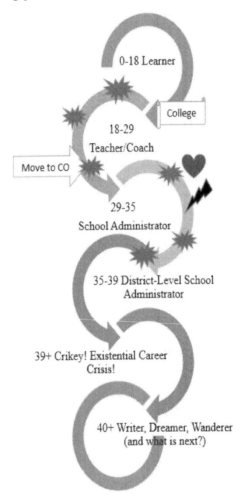

Your Turn: Potential Areas: Life, Career, Love, Health, Faith

Over the last five years I have come upon a rather startling, empowering and, for the classic overachiever that I am, quite nauseating conclusion. You can be very, very good at something you are not passionate about. In fact, you can be highly regarded at something you can't stand doing. All of my life I have thought that if you were good at something, it was, at least in part, because you enjoyed it and wanted to be doing it. I was a very good teacher and changed the lives of many students for the better. Being an Assistant Principal and Principal was a lot of hard work and I made an important difference in the lives of the students and teachers at those schools by showing compassion and an uncanny skill for building effective systems. As a District-level Math Director, I focused on the direction of math instruction that impacted thirty thousand students and a thousand teachers. I was very good at what I did, and I enjoyed it. It wasn't until recently when I received a compliment on work that was mentally and emotionally tedious that I realized the truth. I was (am) devastated. I was so fortunate to have always enjoyed my work – always had a calling, always knew my career path – and had always been good at it. But now I know that one can successfully complete tasks and apply oneself to doing "a good job" for the sake of professionalism, responsibility, obligation, work ethic, or kindness, and not give a lick about the work itself. Sarah Gundle, a clinical psychologist in New York City, tells us from her research that "for well-being, we need to feel satisfaction from accomplishment, and joy" from the pleasure of doing what we are doing. And when we don't feel that satisfaction and joy we may need to dive into something new.

Something exciting and scary. Trying something new means taking a risk. In Great Britain they sell giant letter "L" stickers for your car. Being Yankees, we had to ask what this was all about. It is a "Learner" sticker that you are expected to put on your car if you are just learning to drive. I love this. I feel like I want to sew one of these on all of my shirts, quit my job and spend my time learning stuff with a giant disclaimer on my chest. Let's be deliberate learners. Put on your "learner's permit" and be a deliberate rookie, which may mean that you are not good at what you do, though you will enjoy it tremendously. This takes great courage.

Complete Activity 1.17.2 below. Once you have finished the activity, take a nice hard look at the middle section of the diagram. These things indicate your path and how close to finding it and following it you are.

Activity 1.17.2 What You Love to Do Best

Ken Robinson defines *The Element* as the "place where the things you love to do and things that you are good at come together."

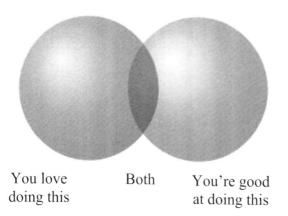

You love   Both   You're good
doing this   at doing this

1)   List all the things that you *LOVE* doing.
Be as exhaustive as you can. This is not just
about your work life. If you love to bust out
Gospel music in the shower, list it here.

1)   List all the things you are good at.
Again, this is not just about your work life. If
you make a mean Mac & Cheese, list it here.

2)   Now,   consider your two lists together. I want you to really challenge your thinking here. Place all your items into the two circles of the Venn diagram below. Think very carefully about the items that go in the overlapping section. These are items that you LOVE and ARE GOOD AT.

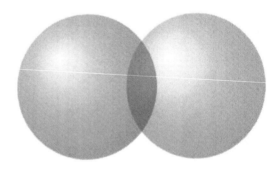

Hopefully, you really listed things you love to do – even if you haven't done them for years or cannot find the time to do them now. If you did not list drawing on your list, but still remember the joy of spending hours sitting in a tree drawing the leaves, then go back and do the activity again with that feeling of joy in mind.

Let us take the results from our activity and find our path, shall we? One of the things "I love" is to read Oprah's magazine. Two of the things I am good at is understanding and helping people. As it turns out, I read the magazines and books to understand myself and others better so that I can both be a better person myself and help others. This is where the circles overlap for me. So, one part of my path for right now (and remember that this my path *for now*; it may turn and wander another direction later) is to use what I have learned from what I love doing (reading *Oprah*) to help people. I think I'll write a book.

I'd like to say that this was clear for me, but it was not. It was much more gut based. "I must get this book out of my head" was more like it, but, when debriefing the first draft with a friend, she asked me what my goal was for this book. It became very clear that I am doing this to help people who are struggling or will struggle with the same things I have struggled with before and during the writing of this book. Doing the activity helped me narrow down how I can use my talents and my interests to make positive changes in myself, my life, your life and this world.

That example makes it seem so stinking easy to flush out your heart's desire. As I have explained earlier, having a thought and bringing it to fruition can take time, courage and support. It can be very scary to consider finding and joining your path, especially if you get the feeling that you are very far away from it now. Remember, this is not just about your career (though for many people their careers are the manifestation of their path). We will return to the obstacles and overcoming them with support later in the Demi-Chapter. For now, we will start with uncovering your path.

Look at the items you placed in the center, overlapping part of the circle diagram. Do you see any specific pairings? Maybe you see "dogs" (LOVE) and "cleaning up poo" (GOOD AT). Your path may lead you to a dog rescue as a volunteer, employee or owner. Be creative in your matches. You may uncover (or need help uncovering) jobs, careers, volunteer opportunities or hobbies that you did not even know existed. Just because you have shoved it away in the cedar closet of your mind to be gnawed upon by moths of regret, doesn't mean you can't pull it out and do it now. Look around for the little things trying to get your attention – what gives you a little tweak, a nod, a vibe or makes you cock your head like a listening dog. Those clues are leading you to the next best things.

My new favorite literary crush and author of *For the Love*, Jen Hatmaker, promises that "someone will pay you to do what you love.

You might have a job you hate, doing work you don't care about, and you are stuck in inertia. (Oh! Me, me! That's me!) Is there a job description with your name on it?" My job may be someone's dream job. I do my job well, but not with as much heart as I wish I did. None of us mean to lose our passion for our work. Todd Henry, the author of *The Accidental Creative*, believes that mediocrity is not intentional and few of us start the day with a pledge to "deliver a steaming pile of crap at work today." It just happens when we wander off our path or ignore the promptings of the fairies. Sometimes it takes stepping in one of those steaming piles of crap (yours or someone else's) to help you realize how far afield you are. This is a career example because that happens to be my current crisis, but the path permeates all facets of our lives. Your steaming pile of crap may come up in any area of life. The fairies are weird like that. For example, one day I sat in two morning meetings where the attendees were so passionate that there was no structure to the conversation, and it could have gone on for hours. I realized that I envied these people. They used to be my "tribe" but more and more they are not. My tribe is now the "Burnt Out and Professionally Discouraged" tribe. I know other people who should be in my current tribe, but the impassioned geniuses in these meetings are members of my former "I Am an Educator and I Can Make a Difference" tribe. My work has become a checklist of things to do, assignments to finish, regular communications to complete, because I am a professional, but not because I could talk all day about my work. It made me sad that this steaming pile of crap was mine. I asked myself: Is there anything that you could talk about for hours without structure or an agenda? Now I will ask you. Is there anything that you could talk about for hours without structure or agenda? If the answer is yes, that thing had best be in your circle for LOVE to do. And probably needs to be in the middle paired with something else that closely resembles a job.

How do we know when we are on "The Path"? I would suggest that it feels right. I know, that's a terribly squishy answer, but even Mr. Spock advised his younger self we should "give up logic and do what feels right" (*Star Trek*, 2012). Gretchen Rubin advises (in case you've got a problem with Spock) to not give your gut short shrift. She described in *The Happiness Project* that she was "haunted by an uncomfortable feeling that I wasn't doing what I was 'supposed' to be doing." Now there are two definitions of "supposed to be doing." The first is your path - where you feel the best and make the best contribution to this world. The second is that nasty follow-the-rules-young-lady "supposed to" and that just doesn't apply in this situation. Sir Ken counsels us that "when people are in their element, they connect with something fundamental to their sense of identity, purpose, and well-being."

As you consider the questions in activity

1.17.3, think about what you do – or maybe used to do – that puts you in the zone. What is it that you do smoothly, confidently and with an almost obsessive intensity? Not that you will always be perfectly in the zone, but if there is something that slides you into the zone, that is an important consideration for your pathfinding. I love writing this book for you. I mean, I flat out, out-of-my-mind love writing this for you. All day I pick up things and think about how I could turn that into something that one of my beloved readers might benefit from. Some days I sit at the computer and the words pour out of me like milk from a dairy cow. Some days ... I stare at the computer and think about sandwiches (come on inspiration!). BUT (and that's a really big but), I know that this is my path because the zone is available to me. Activities we love don't leave us exhausted after ten minutes. Sometimes we get exhausted just thinking about the energy sucker activities that we do that are not path friendly. If you get exhausted just thinking about getting out of bed to eventually do *that* … well, maybe *that* isn't on your path anymore. Your path (the circle center activities) fill you with energy, even if you are physically exhausted. My first full days of writing were ten-hour marathons, but you know what? I felt amazing and energized and so excited about the "work." That was yet another huge waving flag telling me that this is precisely what I need to be doing. This is my path, for now.

Activity 1.17.3 Not Quite 20 Questions

(adapted from Todd Henry's 2015 Colorado Association of School Executive's Conference)

Here are some guiding questions to help you identify if you are on your path or if something in your circle center (or in your heart) is what you should start doing immediately, unless sooner is more convenient. When you ask yourself these questions, whether you are writing answers or just thinking on them, listen carefully to your gut and your spine. If you feel a flutter of excitement or a twinge of energy on a certain question, pay attention! There is something there that you need to apply to your search for your path.

1) What is your clearly articulated guiding principle?

2) Is what you are doing now aligned with that?

3) Is there anything in your circle center that aligns to that?

4) Are there things that you are doing now that are better suited to people with a passion for it?

5) Are you using your gifts?

6) What gives you irrational hope?

7) What fills you with compassionate anger?

8) Is there something you

want desperately to fix?

9)   What do you love to do all day?

10) What are you so passionate about that you are willing to do it all day?

11) When you are doing something you love, does the rest of the world pass away timelessly?

12) What idea are you carrying around and putting off?

13) What gift could you give the world that you do not want to be buried with you?

14) Is your best work out there?

15) What do you need to do now so that your body of work represents you and something you are proud of?

16) What should you be doing now so you do not have regrets later?

I have tried not to put über lengthy quotes in this book, but as we start the discussion of why we often lose our path I wanted to pull powerful excerpts from Paulo

Coelho's introduction to *The Alchemist*. The obstacles that impede our progress on or towards our path come in four basic categories. Though they may look different for you in the details, they are the same for us all.

> *"However, we don't all have the courage to confront our own dream. Why? There are four obstacles. ...*
> *First: we are told from childhood onward that everything we want to do is impossible. We grow up with this idea, and as the years accumulate, so too do the layers of prejudice, fear and guilt (vi)."*

It is often an insurmountable feat to buck the system of societal expectations. In the U.S. we are taught that life is about money and stuff. The culture we live in says that we aren't supposed to leave financially stable and successful careers to pursue the "soft" goals in our lives – passion, happiness, meaningfulness, joy. For those of us in service fields that already focus on the human experience rather than large salaries, we are under even more scrutiny when we feel we must find more meaningful or joyful work. When I say out loud that I am considering quitting my job in education (not like I got into it for the money anyway) to write a book and help the homeless, people adopt that voice they use with the mentally ill, chronically dreaming or distant relatives – "oh, isn't that nice" with the pat on the arm and the discrete roll of the eyes that says, "next, she'll start talking about growing organic quinoa in her back yard.

Let's go find the punch." The real goal here is to find the balance of feeling secure financially, having a rewarding work life, and feeling like you are making a difference in the world. Gretchen Rubin cited peoples' biggest worries as "financial anxiety, health concerns, job insecurity, and having to do tiring and boring chores." Well, we are talking about how to fix all of those things. If you can find a way to support yourself and have an outlet for your creative and charitable energies, then your health will improve, provided that you maintain balance, and your sense of meaning in your life will also improve without killing your financial security. Sir Robinson reminds us that "to be in your Element, it isn't necessary to drop everything else and do it all day, every day. For some people, at some stages in their lives, leaving their current jobs or roles to pursue their passions simply isn't a practical position." Pinterest is filled with part-time passioneers with day jobs. Would that be enough for you?

This next activity will ask you to consider one of your passions and how you can include it in your current life. What do you need in order to be able to surrender yourself to your path?

Activity 1.17.4 Part-time Passioneer

Pick one of your passions from activity 1.17.2 (the circle center).

1) How much time per week do you need to do this activity to feel

fulfilled?

2) Can this activity be done on the side? What would that look like?

3) Is there any way you could turn this activity into an income source? What contacts do you already have who could help with this?

4) What do you need to do to feel value from this activity? Do you need to be published? Put on display? Does it need to help others? Do you need a tangible product?

5) When can you start?

"... If we have the courage to disinter the dream, we are then faced by the second obstacle: love. We know what we want to do, but are afraid of hurting those around us by abandoning everything in order to pursue our dream. ...We do not realize that those who genuinely wish us well want us to be happy and are prepared to accompany us on that journey." (Paulo Coelho)

Those that love us can see how unhappy we are when off our path. It may require sacrifice on the part of everyone, but the rewards of you being happy and healthy will far outweigh the pay cut, the lessened time per week with them, or the ceasing of being at home in exchange for a few hours in flying lessons. Love encourages and supports. If your loved ones argue against your pursing your passion it may be that they do not feel that they are able to pursue theirs.

Work together to figure out how all of you can make the changes needed to pursue your individual paths while staying interdependent and increasing your happiness. This might take some work and a sense of vulnerability, but it is worth it. Will and I are both fiercely independent and I am financially neurotic, so for both of us to offer that the other could leave their work to finish their goal (he, his doctorate, and me, this book series) is an incredible willingness to support the other's passion and path. Neither of us have accepted the offer (yet) but knowing that our partner is willing to make that sacrifice to support us on our path is empowering and reassuring.

Be willing to accept that when you first start, you may not be able to go professional with your passion. That may not be your path. Or it might be. There are stories all over the world of people who hit a sweet spot with their first attempt at following their path. But remember, just like you, whatever they produced has been rattling around in their heads for years. It did not just happen.

I recently talked with a friend about the terrifying prospect of publishing this book. I have all kinds of fears around that next step. The best thing she said to me was around timing. She spent six years writing her book. Her mentor spent two years getting it prepared to be presented to publishers. It doesn't just happen. Often, the path is a nice, long, bumpy, curvy road. Those people who are professionals (and earning a living wage) at their passion are following their paths. Your path may not wander into the professional realm. In America, we have this "go big or go home" mentality that really does taint the beauty of the small but meaningful contribution. My sister earned her Bachelor's degree in art. She painted beautiful paintings of shoes. I loved those paintings. I bought one. It has hung in every home I've had for the last twenty years. She is now a public librarian in a wonderful small town in Ohio. She doesn't paint anymore. She isn't a professional artist, but her art is more to my liking than eighty percent of what I see in professional galleries. Her path wasn't that of a professional artist (at least yet). Her path was to raise two wonderful children and to keep a household with a military father intact. She's done a marvelous job. As her children grow, her youngest will be twelve soon, her path will change. Maybe she will be a professional artist someday, but it doesn't matter – her art has hung in my house for decades. Yes, I have a thing for shoes, but still, it is really good art. The same goes for this book. Whether I make money after it is finished, or I have to beg people to read it, it is still the same book and it is still the product of my passion and my path. It will still be the same book, whether I am deemed a professional writer or not. And I will still be delighted to have written it for you. Any sacrifices I made towards those I love will be understood by my ability to love them at a higher level now that this part of me is happy.

> *"... We come up against the third obstacle: fear of the defeats we will meet on the path."* (Paulo Coelho)

This is just part of the human condition. We fear failure more than any other species. If a dog fails to catch the ball the first time, he simply tries harder the next time or just expects that ball-fetching isn't his strength. Maybe he is the best at critter catching or getting the most bits of shredded cheese that fall from the kitchen counters. The fear of disapproval can stymie us

– even paralyze us. Those people who doubt us may be right – maybe we won't succeed – but maybe they don't know all that you have inside you (Robinson). There are lots of reasons why people hope we fail or predict that we will. It may be jealousy, or it may be out of genuine concern for our well-being. For instance, if you want to leave your $100,000 per year job and start working for $40,000 at a non-profit that stirs your heart, your parents may have a genuine concern for you and your family and your ability to live well and pay your bills. They may have no doubt that you are excited and passionate about the new work; they may not have any doubt that you will excel at the work and feel satisfied and helpful. They do have doubts about your ability to adjust your life to account for a $60,000 reduction in income. If you find yourself in the company of a nay-sayer, ask them what is really behind their concern. You may find that their doubts create an opening for you to explain your preparedness, rethink your plan or grow even closer to the person.

One of the major reasons we do not follow our passion or jump onto our path is that we feel the timing isn't right. Jen Hatmaker reminds us that "the timing is never right. Forget that. It rarely just falls into your lap. You are probably not guaranteed success. This might be a risk. ... We are not created to stand still." You probably know some people who seem to have great jobs, great opportunities, great kids, great ... whatever ... just fall into their laps. I hate those people. Okay, well, hate is too strong. I envy those people. Luckily, I look great in green, so envy works for me. But what I am not seeing is that those people probably worked really hard so that this is just the right time. What looks like happiness delivered on a silver platter has come with strings attached. We don't know anyone's whole story – even our best friend. We aren't in their head every minute of every day (thank God!). Focus on your path, your passion, your life and try to worry less about what "they" say or think. In *Eat, Pray, Love*, yogic text Bhagavad Gita is translated for us to tell us that "it is better to live your own destiny imperfectly than to live an imitation of somebody else's life with perfection." If you are following your instincts, inspiration, and heart, then you are on the right track for you.

> *Then comes the fourth obstacle: the fear of realizing the dream for which we fought all our lives.*
>
> *...The mere possibility of getting what we want fills the soul of the ordinary person with guilt. ...This is the most dangerous of obstacles because it has a kind of saintly aura about it: renouncing joy and conquest. But if you believe yourself worthy of the thing you fought so hard to get, then you become an instrument of God, you help the Soul of the World, and you understand why you are here.* (Coelho, viii)

This is like survivor's guilt. Achiever's guilt. Happiness guilt. As a student of history, it is so interesting to research and start to understand the subtle moirés that come from the hodgepodge of cultural influences. The Puritan work ethic and idea of predetermination show themselves here. It is a fine balance between entitlement and worthiness. I referred to this earlier as the golden handcuffs, the guilt that comes with wanting more out of a life that has already given me so much. Again, I refer to Jen Hatmaker. She reminds us that we "are too vital to lose years to regret or shame or insecurity or fear." Or guilt. It is okay for you to love your life. Flakiness, forgetfulness, fear, insomnia and lots of other great side effects come from the stress that accompanies a lack of enjoyment (Martha Beck). Everyone is due a life of contentment. It opposes nature to think otherwise. One afternoon, after a snowstorm, I was walking around the neighborhood pond. It was beautiful. The creek entering the pond was iced over, but the water was still running at full force. It came to me that nature always finds its way around obstacles. The water bubbled along happily. It did not stop. It did not need a nap because a rock appeared in its way. Do you think the water feels guilty because it overcame an obstacle and made it to the pond? It just followed its path. Find ways to make it happen and open your viewpoint to the possibilities in your life. The next activity will help you invite a vision of your path into your heart and mind. This activity is not of my creation. It is taken directly from Martha Beck.

Activity 1.17.5 Inviting the Right One In

(taken directly from Martha Beck's "It's All About What You Do with Your Breakthrough" in the August 2014 issue of *The Oprah Magazine*.)

"FORM No. 1 Fill in the blanks below as honestly as you can. Don't hold back. Plan to trash this form later so you can

write without feeling like anyone is judging.
To start, think of the most stuck person you
know. Ready? Begin.

1. This person is getting in his/her own
   way by being so_____.

2. This person could really break
   through if he/she would only _____.

3. This person is actually just afraid of
   _____.

4. If this person knew what was good for
   him/her, he/she would _____.

5. Meanwhile, I also know someone
   brave enough to do anything he/she
   wants. The quality that makes this
   person so amazing is ____.

6. I'm grateful that this person didn't
   give in, but instead behaved in a way
   that was _____.

7. If I had this person as a mentor, I'd
   have the guts to _____.

8. If this person were mentoring me,
   what I'd love to hear him/her say is

_____."

"FORM No. 2 Complete form 1 before reading form 2. *"Now fill out Form 2 by copying each answer from Form 1 into the corresponding blank below. Don't think as you write and don't tweak your words. If you really want a breakthrough, faithfully copy what you wrote.*

1. I can think of time when I was (copy your answer to question 1 in Form 1) _____.

2. I really need to just (copy your answer to question 2 in Form 1) ____.

3. I'm really just afraid of (copy your answer to question 3 in Form 1) _____.

4. If I knew what was good for me, I would (copy your answer to question 4 in Form 1) _____.

5. On the other hand, what makes me so amazing is that I'm (copy your answer to question 5 in Form 1) _____.

6. I can recall times when I've had the

courage to behave in a way that was (copy your answer to question 6 in Form 1) _____.

7. Deep down, I have everything it takes to (copy your answer to question 7 in Form 1) _____.

8. My true self is always guiding and comforting me. Right now, it is saying (copy your answers to question 8 in Form 1) _____.

Now read through Form 2. Open your mind to ways in which it might be accurate. Take your own advice. And see if your viewpoint doesn't start to expand into something greater than you ever imagined.

Alright, we are all filled with purpose and terrified about the next steps. How do we reach out for support? Identify the people in your life who can help you. Look for both the warm-fuzzy supporters and the critical-friend supporters. I am not a big fan of the critical friend title, but it does describe the job pretty well. You need people who think that anything you create is absolutely marvelous and inspire you to keep going. Then you need the realistic people who aren't afraid to tell you that you do, actually, look fat in that dress. This may require networking – yuck! It may require research, cold calls, vulnerability, admitting you don't know what you are doing and … gasp!... asking for help. And not just "Dear Lord, help me" – though that has its own power, to be sure. I hate networking. I don't like to ask for help, I do not like feeling out of my depth. However, I had to swallow my pride and admit that I do not know anything about publishing. In spite of my fear, I have reached out to people I hardly know to ask about their experiences and ask for advice. I am, gulp, networking. I have an exciting list of connections and ideas now. I have asked some of my warm-fuzzy friends to read this manuscript. Like faith and inspiration, the more I practice taking help, the better I get at asking for help. And, surprisingly, the more I feel that my path is illuminating before me. I wish you joy in your daily work, work that gives you the thrill and energy to live your life with meaning.

Demi-Chapter XVIII: Fear

Face your fears. Fear is specific to each individual, yet completely universal. Everyone has fears. Fear can manifest itself as impatience, intolerance, impertinence, aggression, withdrawal or inaction. Fear can sit in the back of your mind like a shadow for years without you even noticing it. But once it starts preventing you from doing and being and loving yourself – it is time to shine the light on it. We all have it and we all have to face it if we wish to find our best selves and our best lives.

Why do we fear? We fear things that we cannot control. Fear is a hard-wired reptilian brain function that has allowed us to survive long enough to become who we are. Fear is a security service. Our own personal ADT, watching out for us so we can go about doing higher-level-species-like things. However, like the Incredible Hulk, our fear centers can get a little overzealous in our fast-paced, hyped-up, adrenalized world. One key difference between the Western world's modern philosophy and the ancient Eastern philosophies is the sense of control. The more we think we can control the world around us, the more we fear that we cannot. The more we fear that we cannot control the world around us, the more we stress about how our not controlling the world around us will negatively impact our lives. The more we stress out, the more we try to control all of the variables. A fear of failure is the fear that we cannot control the outcome, we cannot make ourselves the winner of all things.

We also fear out of a sense of being wronged, intimidated or minimized. This loops back to not being in control, but it has more of a social context; we cannot control the behavior of others. I, for instance, often find myself fearful that Will and I will never marry. Unfortunately for his girls, especially the eldest, this fear manifests itself as frustration and impatience, a sense of invisibility and a perceived lack of value. Rather than focusing on my behavior or even his, I focus on things I might be able to control that might be obstacles standing in the way of our moving forward with our life. Notice I did not say that I ever asked him if these are obstacles. Because I know it is an empty fear, I am too embarrassed to bring it up. (Note to self: Nice Bright Red Flag). It is completely inappropriate to blame the girls' and even if it were true - which it is not – and I think we shan't take the foray into misplaced blame just now - it leads us nowhere, as much fear does. My fear is something only I can control. My fear of the consequences of the behavior of others provides me with no answers, no comfort, no truth and no strength. We can only control our behaviors. In *Pride and Prejudice*, Jane Austin's character, Elizabeth, tells Mr. Darcy that "My courage always rises with every attempt to intimidate me." You, too, my friend, must find this courage when you are intimidated, devalued or feel less than you are due to your interpretation of the behaviors of others.

Activity 1.18.1 Why do you fear?

1. Think of some event or situation in your life that holds fear for you. It could be an upcoming change at work, it could be a presentation at your local Men's' or Women's' club, it might be a child's pending nuptials or a dear friend's upcoming medical procedure. Think of something that carries with it fear. You will probably know it by a constricting of the chest or a need to cry when you think of it.

2. Say out loud or write down here what

you fear about or from this situation. This is private, and no one need ever see it but you. What thought constricts your chest? What terrifies you most about this situation? What is the utmost worst thing that could possibly happen?

3. *Why* does what you wrote above bring you fear? *Why* would it change your life? *Why* would you or another person suffer because of it happening? *Why* is it worthy of so much anxiety?

The why we fear clearly aligns closely with the what we fear. What do we fear? How long have you got? We are going to focus on what I call the life fears versus the day-to-day fears. The day-to-day fears are the more mundane fears and worries: spiders, being late for work, kid's grades, cellulite, et cetera. We are going to focus on the life fears: unknown, failure, humiliation, and regret. You know, the easy stuff that can be solved in a few quick pages.

One of our first steps in overcoming our

fear is to figure out to what we are reacting and why we are so afraid. Activity 1.18.1 will walk you through three steps to help you identify why you carry the fears you have.

The unknown. A classic fear. We fear what we do not know. We fear that we cannot predict and control the future. We do not know what might happen if we did "x," whereas, we believe we know what will happen if we continue to do "y." What I would like you to think about is, can you really know what will happen if you continue to do "y"? I am going to suggest that the only thing that will happen if you continue to do "y" is that you will continue to yearn for the something more that comes with doing "x." For example, I can continue to go to my job and do the daily work out of a fear of not knowing what will happen to my finances if I quit and become a barista while I finish this book. What I suspect (I do not know) is that each day I go to work will be just like the day before that and the day before that and I will become more and more detached from my work. What I do not know is if I continue to go to work will I be asked to resign because I've become so ineffective? Will I have a heart attack from the stress? Will I be asked to resign because the leadership has decided to "go in a different direction"? We cannot predict stability in this world. Maybe we cannot predict what will happen if we make the leap, but we also cannot predict what might happen if we don't. You can't know what might happen. You can't fear that you might get hurt, that you might struggle, that you might fail a little bit, that you might have to answer some tough questions.

You shouldn't hold yourself back because you are afraid or because you have been hurt. Just as you cannot know what bad things might come if you leap, you also cannot know what beautiful, wonderful, exciting and inspiring things might come that you will miss if you stand still. The beauty of the unknown is that it may be filled with the life you have always dreamed of having.

I fear failure. When it comes to examining our lives, I believe that the most common fear is the fear of failure. Failure can look very different to each person. For some, feeling imperfect is the same as failure. For some, thinking that others will think he/she is incompetent is failure. Some feel that a well-planned event that turns out differently than planned is failure. Dan Stanford, BBC journalist, has been quoted all over the internet saying, "experience is what you get when you don't get what you want." For many, this is also a definition for failure and a recipe for fear.

Fear of failure comes in many forms, all of which return to the fact that we cannot control anything outside of ourselves. Each of us defines failure based on our own personal history and hopes for our lives. I have a deep-seeded fear of being poor. I was raised fairly middle-working class. Yet, I have a strangely powerful fear of losing control of my finances, of making mistakes, of ending up having to "worry about money," which is of course, ironic, considering how much I worry about money now. As the "bread winner," the loss of income can be scary. One of my promises to myself is to stop making weird decisions based on my fears about money. I have to seriously structure my money-thinking in order to not be unduly influenced by my fears about not having enough money. There may be a cultural or historical basis for our fears. Or there may not be. Fear does not have to have a logical base to it. We base fear of failure on what our families will think, what our bank account reports, what our title reads.   Shaking off the American success-ethic is tough.

People are often afraid to take care of their own happiness, fearing it will make them look naïve, selfish or make others feel bad about themselves. In our ever-expanding world, it is hard to keep a new endeavor quiet. A failure can hit social media in less time than it takes us to slam the car door and scream out loud. You need to identify what failure looks like for you so that you can make your peace with it. Once you know, then you take control of your fear and you can stop calling it failure and start calling it living your life bravely. "Blowing out your life can be life changing," says Oprah. It can also be terrifying.   Fear can make us anxious, shy, forgetful and unwilling to take the risks we need to take because we are afraid that we will fail ourselves, our loved-ones or someone important in our fields.

The first step around this fear of failure is to identify what failure looks like for you.

Activity 1.18.2 will ask you to think back on the most painful failure you can recall and try to pinpoint specific details to help you counteract those fears in your future.

Activity 1.18.2 Failure to ID

Think about a time you "failed." If you can stand it, pick the most painful failure you have in your past.

1. Describe what happened. What did you do? Who else was involved? What did they do?

2. What did you feel? If you can, immerse yourself in the moment and describe the physical reactions and emotional feelings you had related to what you considered to be your failure.

3. Who else was involved in your feeling of failure? What did he or she say to incite your feelings of failure? Pinpoint specific word triggers that promoted your feelings of failure in this moment. Record those here.

4. Do you still feel the pain of this event? If yes, what stays with you? What feelings,

thoughts and actions reinforce your feeling that this was a failure?

5. If you had the chance to "undo" this failure, what would you do? What point would you return to? Is there something you would have done differently? Is there something you can do to change this from a failure to just an event in your life?

Humiliation, another outcast relative of loss of control, haunts most of us. Somewhere in our past we were either the subject of humiliating taunts or watched it happen to another (maybe even participated). The fear that we cannot control what other people think or say about us and, ultimately, that others will believe what is said, like dominos falling, often stops us in our tracks. I have to admit that I have avoided often (and to some extent still do) things out of sheer pride and fear of humiliating myself. My attempts at downhill skiing are a good example. I took a class. Three full Saturdays of lessons with a nice group. I was the only one who could not master exiting the ski lift and staying upright for the whole of the kiddy hill. I was black and blue and completely embarrassed. No one directly laughed at me. In fact, I was left behind entirely. No one was even around to see me, but it was so discouraging that the fear of it happening again still keeps me off the slopes. Add that to the fact that I can fall down and slide the length of a snowy hill on my butt for completely free with no need to face the traffic, pay the lift ticket and stand in line for the privilege to do it in public, and I'm content to never try it again. Clearly, I haven't mastered this be-brave-about everything lesson. But I am aware of my fear and also know that skiing is a rather small bit in my life, so I have prioritized it way on down the list of fears I need to tackle right now.

Fear of feeling embarrassed is only erased by faith in yourself and your knowledge that you believe in your worth and no one can take that away from you. Yes, we will fall down, and we will fail to meet our own expectations and others might judge us, but when we can appreciate ourselves and our courage for trying, then we will no longer be subject to the fear of humiliation. I know that everyone falls when learning to ski. I know that it makes no difference to anyone if I cannot ski. This is about self-humiliation – I am embarrassed that I live in Colorado and I can't figure out how to ski. It is a combination of fears that are entirely fabricated in my mind. These fears have taken the joy out of trying to learn to ski. Clearly, I need to lighten up. As Oscar Wilde said, "life is too important to be taken seriously." So is anyone's opinion of you. Or of me. But I am sticking with my falling for free plan.

Finally, let's examine regret, the final fear frontier. These are the voyages of the Starship Should've Done. We explored the strange planet of past-tense regrets in the earlier Demi-Chapter on letting go. What we fear are future-tense regrets – those that haven't happened yet, but just might. Again, a fear of not knowing and controlling the future pulls the strings on this puppet. We create stress around what we might or might not worry about in the future. When we fear that we might have regrets, we are paralyzed and cannot make decisions or take risks. I know that I've stayed in place because I feared what might or might not happen. I intentionally held myself back from trying and growing. And to what end? Here I am still asking the same questions and wanting the same things. When we worry, we feel the pain twice. The same is true in any decision. If you stand still because of fear of future regrets, you make the conscious decision not to grow into your life.

Eleanor Roosevelt said that "we must do the things we think we cannot do." We must also do the things we think we might do imperfectly. We might have to do things before having all of the information. The key, I have learned, is to trust that you are making the best decision with the information you have *at the moment*. That is the best you can do. I am going to reference a not-so-deep example. I am not minimalizing our traumas and struggles, and I don't want to trivialize someone's deepest sorrows in my example either. It's a simple everyday example. I have a friend who recently bought a new Toyota Highlander in a beautiful color. It is absolutely gorgeous. She was worried about whether she had picked the right color, and would she regret it. I assured her that it was a perfect color but mostly that she chose the best color that was available based on all of the information she had at the time. Considering she was also having a baby within a few weeks; I think she made a perfect choice and spending more time finding a color she didn't worry about seemed like a waste of precious brain cells.

A few years ago, during the

counseling sessions I worked through after my divorce, I learned this for myself. I had so many future regrets; what if this happens again? What if I make the same poor choices again? But the truth of the matter is that the choices I made cannot be changed and I made them with the best of intentions, with all the information I had at the time. I would do the same again. Does that ever prevent a potential mistake? Does that ever provide us with all the information that we might need? No. But it does assure us that we are making decisions without future regrets. It is the best we can do and preventively beating yourself up or suspending your life out of fear that you might regret a decision only robs you of the joy (or necessary learning) that may come your way. You don't know everything that is in the plan for you. You cannot and will not ever know everything.

You have to trust in yourself, God, and the plan the universe has for you. If you make a mistake it is because there is a lesson in there for you to learn. There is never a regret to be had. Every action has an equal and opposite reaction. If you begin to accept your life and the have faith in yourself, then there is never anything to regret. There is never anything to fear. Spending your energy on whether or not you should worry about something that may or may not happen is not a very green use of your energy. Go hug your dog or take a walk with your children (or vice versa) or clean out your refrigerator with all that extra energy.

How we fear also looks different for all of us. I fear in my head. First, I feel it in my guts – that churning sensation. Then, a tidy army of little terrible Jackie's, all suited up like legal-eagles, lines up in my head and there starts a very organized and well-thought-out, albeit it mostly crazy-talk, legal argument about the logical nature of the fear. It really is quite fascinating to listen to and the suits are fabulous, but it is a little too *Being John Malkovich* for me. Luckily, I can recognize it now and, usually, get it cut off by the end of the opening arguments. I have learned, and use the knowledge often, that the conversations I practice in my head are not what is going to happen in real life and are more the stuff of Hollywood. I have a fight response when it is an emotional fear. If it is a physical fear, like, say, breaking my face by trying to learn how to skateboard at 40, then I am a flight kind of gal. Actually, if I am being truthful with y'all, what I really want is a big stoic emotional henchman who just looms, cross-armed and intimidating behind me, fending off the fear before it even gets close to me. I want an emotional Oddjob, only one that looks like Dwayne Johnson. What fears can stand up to The Rock? Yes. I want a big emotional Dwayne Johnson henchman who will keep me safe. There. I said it. I think I might make it so. Ha! Fears be warned!

How do you fear? Notice from my example that you may not react to all fears the same way. Try this next activity to home in on some of your fear responses. This one is rather long, so you might want to get some chocolate before you start.

Activity 1.18.3 How you fear matters

I am going to ask you to think about your fears in categories: emotional, family, professional and physical. For each fear, circle the item that best describes the way you respond to each fear. It may not be exact but pick the closest reaction to your own. I have added suggested prompts to each fear to help you identify your response, but you may also want to think of a situation that triggers your fear response to help you truly identify what is happening when you respond to fear.

A. Emotional: you are out shopping and that see your friends went out to eat and did not invite you to accompany them. Your fear response is to:

1. Fight: You feel angry. You want to

march right up to them up and tell them they don't deserve you for a friend!

2. Flight: You feel it is best to just ignore it. It was probably just a mistake. You don't want to upset them by pointing it out, so you turn around and leave the mall, before they see you.

3. Freeze: You aren't sure what to do. You are upset, but your anxiety about looking desperate makes you feel stuck and indecisive.

4. Hide and seek: You dive behind a pillar and try to get a better look. Can you hear what they are saying? You call another mutual friend who isn't there and ask if she was invited. You do not confront them, but you hold onto this nugget of information until you might need it again.

5. Assume positive intent: You shrug it off and assume that there was a perfectly good reason why you were not included. Maybe they are planning your birthday party! Or you missed the email. You do not approach them because that might make them uncomfortable when there

is no need for that. You are not one to let a potential oversight ruin your day. You go buy some awesome shoes.

B. Family: Your daughter went out with friends last night and is not at home in her bed in the morning when you wake up.

1. Fight: You feel angry. You don't fear she is in danger, you fear she is making bad decisions and disrespecting your authority. You call her cell phone immediately and tell her to get her little tush home right now.

2. Flight: You are afraid she is in trouble, but you are also afraid that you are limiting her freedom if you check on her. You need a distraction. You'll do the laundry and just wait for her to come home. You're sure it is fine; she probably just didn't want to wake you up by calling or texting last night. When she comes home you don't mention it.

3. Freeze: You aren't sure what to do. You are sick with worry that she is hurt or in trouble, but your anxiety about being an overprotective

parent makes you feel stuck and indecisive.

4. Hide and seek: You start texting her friends and her friends' parents. You ask your other daughters if they know where she is. You do not call her cell phone until the last resort.

5. Assume positive intent: You know and trust your daughter, but also want to be sure she is safe. You send her a text to confirm that she is safe. If she does not respond in a short period of time, you calmly call the house of her friend. Once you know that everything is all okay, you plan a calm and rational conversation with her when she returns home to help her understand the importance of keeping you informed and you will work together to determine future consequences if it happens again.

C. Professional: A recent presentation at work did not go well and your boss is asking for more work to be done to bolster the next presentation. This is the fourth revision he has requested, and you feel you have already given him what he is asking for.

1. Fight: You feel angry and resentful. You want to march right into his office and resign. You are tired of being unappreciated. If he wants you to stay, he needs to be clearer in his communication   and appreciation.

2. Flight: You feel it is best to just redo the assignment again. You'll try to get it closer to what you think he wants. There isn't any point in asking about it or causing conflict. You don't want to upset him by pointing out that you have already done these things and you don't want to risk losing your job over this – it isn't worth that.

3. Freeze: You aren't sure what to do. You are upset, but your anxiety about losing your job makes you feel stuck and indecisive. You just sit at your desk and stare at the PowerPoint on the computer screen.

4. Hide and seek: You slink back to your desk and call a colleague. Is he doing this to her too? What does she think he wants? You rework the presentation, getting advice from others, not your boss, along the way.

5. Assume positive intent: After a deep breath, you understand that your supervisor is trying to help you put your best foot forward on this next presentation by giving you feedback for how to improve your presentation. You take the feedback and create your best presentation yet.

D. Physical: Your friend invites you on a sky-diving trip you aren't sure you want to attend and cannot afford.

1. Fight: You feel angry and resentful. You tell her it is dangerous, and she has put you in a bad place because she knows you can't afford it.

2. Flight: "Oh, Hell no." And tell him to never ask you again.

3. Freeze: You aren't sure what to do. You want to stay included but you are terrified by the idea and strapped for cash. You stall until it is too late to say yes.

4. Hide and seek: You pretend you did not hear the invitation and then look up the death rates on Google in order to justify your "no."

5. Assume positive intent: Your friend has done this before and wants to share this "exhilarating experience" with you. You have heard that the dangers are not too bad, statistically, but still feel uneasy about accepting. You ask your friend to talk to you about it, the risks, the costs and the fun of going. Then you feel comfortable telling him whether you will go or not and know that it will be okay if you decline the invitation.

Look at your responses, or the responses to your own personal situations. Consider whether this is the way you would usually respond in this type of fear situation. Make a generalization for how you respond to each: emotional, professional, family and physical fears.

To overcome these fears, you need to both identify how you respond and create a way to offset the fears through an affirmative mantra, physical movement or other distractor. As I mentioned above, I use a mental talking point that no matter how many times I run a conversation through my head, it never turns out that way and it is a waste of time to rehash the imaginary scenario over and over again. Some wise guy once said to make the fear your friend; another guy (I think it might have been in a movie) said to make fear your slave. I don't think I will go that far. I think I will suggest that you make fear your weekly coupon mailer – use it when you think it is helpful and recycle it when it serves no other useful purpose.

How do we go about that? I have helped to raise three girls and taught or mentored hundreds more. I know that I cannot control them or their worlds and, yet, I stubbornly attempt to schedule and plan with them in mind. Herding cats would be child's play compared to coordinating young women. Yet, mostly, I don't fear them anymore. I (mostly) don't fear their disapproval, their criticism, or their anger. I suspect that they complain about me to their friends, their mother, their grandmother, but they absolutely have that right. Other than my "this conversation won't happen like this" mantra, I also lean heavily on "this too shall pass," "God has a plan for me" and "It is what it is." I do have to admit that I cannot always mental my way out of my fear.

Some fears are recurring and there is not a one-time fix. It is an all-the-time fix. That doesn't mean you cannot overcome the fear. You may have a fear of public speaking rooted in a fear of humiliation with a fear of failure chaser. You may be able to get through the first speech by picturing the whole audience is in its nickers. That may not work for the second group when it is a bunch of stodgy executives from your company that you most definitely do not want to see in their nickers. The trick is to have a toolbox of ways to get right to the root of it and if you cannot abolish it forever, at least pack it away for the season.

If your natural tendency is towards the

fight response, try to identify what you can do to diffuse your emotions until you are thinking more clearly. This doesn't mean that you shouldn't address the fear in the situation head-on. It means that you should perhaps not make the situation worse with the other humans involved by racing in with your hair on fire without thinking it through first.

If your responses tend towards the flight response, then work to identify what makes you want to flee from rather than face the fear. Paolo Coelho wrote "Fear of suffering is worse than the suffering itself." Sometimes it is better to give the fear space. Ignoring it all together only leaves you open for nagging doubts or building resentment about the situation. Even worse, if you never face the fear, it will continue to return and may be stronger and stronger each time until you have no alternative but to face it, not as a small kitty but as a roaring lion. It is always better to face fear on your own terms rather than avoid it until it can no longer be ignored. Find a phrase or a go-to person that gives you courage. Acknowledge to yourself that you deserve to be treated well. You deserve the blessings that life has for you and no fear can keep them from you. Nothing will happen in your life without courage.

Those of you who freeze in the face of fear, you need a trigger for action. I freeze in fear when I am nightmaring. If I need to scream in a dream, I completely freeze, and nothing will come out of my mouth. I wake up all panicked and unable to speak. The internal turmoil when we freeze may be considerably worse than any external trouble we are facing. Again, as with the flight responses, you need to have an emergency link. Find a thought or action that helps you get unstuck. Find someone you can text a secret code to that tells that person that you are stuck in fear and need help. Then work with that person prior to a fear situation to identify a trigger question or comment that he/she will send to help you unfreeze. For example, when you are at work and freeze over the on-going conflict between you and the loud colleague in the next cubicle, you might text your partner "F"- for I'm frozen – please help. Because you have worked this out ahead of time your support partner knows that this means you are in a conflict/fear freeze. He/she may respond by texting back, "What do you wish you would say?" That question (for example) should trigger you out of your freeze and help you work out what you want to say and what is the best thing to say. Be sure to work this out ahead of time and with someone who loves and cares for you. You may need it a lot at first and this person needs to be able to be responsive and patient. Once you get the hang of it you may be able to ease yourself out of needing this support at all.

Finally, for those who respond with a hide and seek response you may find yourself in a similar situation as the fliers and freezers above by needing the support of a friend for courage and compassion. My mom calls this "The Ostrich" – and we proudly bury our heads and pretend it never happened – unless of course we need it for ammunition later. The hider response is a little tricky because it falls on the passive aggressive scale in many situations. You are pretending it didn't happen until it is convenient to unleash the pent-up fury, fear and resentment. This allows the fear to fester. I do this, so do not feel that I am throwing stones. I do this and that is exactly why I have to convince myself that the blistering conversation I am planning in my head is not actually going to happen that way. It is why I must force myself to speak up or risk a pestilent sore the size of Vermont. Will is great at helping me get over it. He helps me assess the fear and realize that it isn't logical, address the fear, understand that there is nothing to fear and fight for my self-worth. In a pinch, my officemate, Sam, is also an awesome sounding board for this. Having a trusted person to whom one can, without embarrassment, process fear and doubt, is the ideal solution for the hider. Again, if possible, set this safety net up in advance so the person is ready to support you when you need it.

My friend, Tracy, sent this affirmation to our Hot Yummy Friends Happy Hour group. I hope that this summarizes all the phrases that you need to hear to help you face your fear response and find your way to the positive side of the situation, better for the fear and for the work it took to get over it.

We believe what we tell ourselves. So, tell yourself this: Everything will work out. Things will get better. This too shall pass. The best is yet to come. You are important. You are worthy of great things. You are lovable. You are strong. You can do this. You can be who you really are. The time is now.
-Doe Zantamata,
www.happinessinyourlife.com

Demi-Chapter XIX:
Wait for It

Patience is power.

Patience is not an absence of action;

rather it is "timing"

it waits on the right time to act,

for the right principles

and in the right way.

Fulton J. Sheen

Learn to wait. Or, as the wise folk of the bible advised, patience is a virtue. I would have to say that I most faithfully did not believe this until just the past few years. As a young woman I believed that I had to make my life happen. If I wanted something I worked and worked until I had it and, usually, I did not have to work or wait very long because I worked very hard and was very, very driven. If I wanted it in my career, then I got it. That was not the case in my relationships, but I always just sort of worked at the relationship until it went away and then I worked on the next one until it went away and so on and so forth. I belayed my fears by saying I just hadn't met the right guy yet. And I hadn't. I wasn't consciously waiting per se, I just didn't really have a choice. I tried to control the situations, but I was forced to have patience. Mostly. I didn't like it and I tried to make the relationships happen, but, hey, news flash, relationships do not work that way. My impatience in career worked perfectly until 2009, then I got a nice dose of you-don't-actually-control-any-of-this in that area, too. Hence the lesson on patience. I am still working on it. It is a long lesson.

It was Will and all of the events of the last ten years, orchestrated by the great conductor in the sky, that taught me this important lesson. Slowly, I have let go of control and learned to wait. And by wait, I mean

I have learned to (mostly) let life happen and "roll with it." I have learned to rein in the road-of-life rage that always felt like I was behind the 1942 GMC flatbed truck loaded with chicken crates and maxing out at 35 miles per hour. I still have to remind myself to slow down and breathe and do my best with what I can control, allowing what I cannot control to just take shape. Fear, the great nemesis of happiness, lurks behind all impatience: Fear of being late, fear of consequences, fear of missing something great. As we learned in our study of fear in the last Demi-Chapter, only small amounts of good come from it. There is, however, great value and peace of mind in slowing down, asking yourself what there is to learn from this experience and the wisdom that can be gained from waiting.

I often wondered why I should have to wait for the good things – or anything. I laughed at Woodrow Wilson's sage advice that "all things come to him who waits – provided he knows what he is waiting for." I figured, if I know what I want, why not jump out there and get it? It is the American ethic to go after what you want. It is a part of Eastern philosophy to let what you want come to you. Americans are impatient and determined and wonderfully successful in the world view. Our streets are paved with gold and all that.

Yet, when we really look at our health and happiness, we are not the healthiest and happiest in the world. Our priorities have been so directed by achievement that we, as a nation, are forgetting the value of having family nearby (except at Christmas when we are reminded by Hallmark), taking time to relax and being active, fit and content human beings.

Part of the cause of this is that we are not willing to wait. We get frustrated if there are more than three cars in the drive through line at the *fast* food restaurant (heaven forbid we actually walk into the place). Our blood pressure rises if we sit at a red light for more than one cycle. The post office takes too long to deliver. Cooking is a chore, so we invented the microwave. If the website hasn't loaded in less than a second, we become bored and click somewhere else, which, by the way, only slows our computers down even more. Many of our twenty-five and under generation expect their first job to be a $100,000 salary with six weeks of vacation in a career that is both meaningful and allows them to check on their status on Facebook ten times an hour. Each generation is successively frustrated with the impatience of the ones that come after. I have seen elderly women sit at a bus stop for an hour while I, at 40, pace furiously back and forth for the three minutes until the bus arrives. I have seen gentleman in their 80s just sit on a park bench and watch as people go by. These, my friends, are examples of patience. I have a wonderful friend, Betty, who will cook her prize-winning (at least in my mind) brisket for *twelve hours*. Oh, it is totally delicious, but twelve hours?!

My point with these examples is precisely this: impatience comes from the overcharged fight-or-flight reflex, which kicks in as a survival mechanism during stress, anxiety, depression, entitlement, or boredom. Impatience, while it can produce incredible breakthroughs, high levels of efficient productivity and a sense of effective time management, can also produce high blood pressure, increased cortisol production, increased fat and weight, insomnia, anxiety, sadness (especially if you are waiting for something like a meaningful relationship) and general crankiness. By learning to wait, or to hone your patience skills, you can start to control the only thing in life you can control – yourself and your reaction to things.

When we seek desperately for happiness, which is the true reason why we scurry about like ants at a picnic, we only serve to drive it farther from us. Perhaps Wilson should have said happiness comes to those who wait. Contentment comes to those who *know how* to wait. Even Zeno of Citium, the Greek philosopher said, 2300 years ago, that "well-being is attained by little and little, and nevertheless it is no little thing itself." 2300 years ago, people were striving and pushing and living life impatiently. Westerners have just taken it to a whole new, unhealthy, level.

This may offend some of you who move at light speed all of the time, trying to make your life happen, but I would ask that you consider what would happen if you just stopped for a bit and let life happen.

Gretchen Rubin reminds us that "happiness doesn't always make you <u>feel happy</u>. Activities that contribute to long-term happiness don't always make me feel good in the short term." I think learning to wait is one of these. It may not feel fabulous to wait for years for the perfect job to appear, but if you continue to look and continue to wait rather than rushing from job to job, then you may find important lessons learned and incredible joy in the outcome.

So that's all well and good, you say, but

how do we learn to wait?   In this instant
gratification world – how do we train ourselves
(and our children) to wait? Unfortunately, like
most things, it takes conscious practice.   There
are a few things that you can do to force yourself
to learn patience. Learning patience takes time
– and by that, I mean it takes years and it takes
time from your day. The hardest part of this is
allowing yourself extra time in your packed day
to slow down.   Just like we (in theory) make
time to exercise, meditate, do the dishes, and
read with our children, we need to make time to
practice patience. Try the next activity to focus
on one area of your life where you can start to
develop patience.

Activity 1.19.1 Practice Patience

1. *Consider an area in your life where you
   struggle to have patience. I encourage you to
   start with an easy one and work up to the
   harder   areas.   Write   it   here:*
   _____

2. *Now, think about what is really at the root cause of your impatience and not the target person or behavior. What are you afraid of that is causing your impatience?*

_____ For example, I get impatient in traffic sometimes. I am impatient because the traffic is not moving fast enough. The root cause of my impatience is that I am usually late for something because I did not leave early enough or did not anticipate the degree of traffic. I am impatient because I fear looking irresponsible, insensitive or unprofessional when I am late for an appointment with a person.

3. *What about this event/situation makes you feel impatient? What is the root cause of your impatience?* _____

4. Next, *do the 10-4 Breathing Exercise from Demi-Chapter 1. Take ten 4second inhales.* Forcing your breathing to slow down increases your capacity for patience.

5. *Then, think of a simple step that you can do after the 10-4 breathing exercise every time you are in this impatience situation to help you instigate patience.* In my traffic example above, I do the 10-4 breathing exercise and then I specifically remind myself that first, the fact that I did not leave early enough is not the fault of any other driver on the road; second, if I drive aggressively now I will only make up a few minutes and may endanger myself and others and, third, it is not a big deal if I am late. The world will not end. I will not lose my job. I will apologize and own my mistake. It is fine. Sometimes I need to remind myself repeatedly of this. Sometimes I need to make a phone call to handle my lateness professionally. Usually I just need to chill.

6. *You will use this process every time you are in this impatience situation to help you learn patience. You may want to write it on*

a note card or sticky note, so it is handy for
reference when you need it. As your
patience improves, you may want to repeat
this exercise with more trying situations.
Write the next one here: _____

This activity is a good start for learning patience in small ways, with small daily irritations. Practicing this with your children will help them understand and value patience as well. Developing a short memory trick or routine for children gives them a strategy to fall back on when they are feeling impatient in their lives.

For those of us with large life-decisions that are testing our patience, it can be much harder to find the faith and will to be patient. And being patient is a test of faith. It may be faith in a higher power, or it may be faith in yourself, but either way, it is a test of your faith that things will happen precisely as they are meant to happen. Lord Shelley, harbinger of happy thoughts (that's sarcasm), did lend us promising words for patience in his poem "Ode to the West Wind":

O, wind If Winter comes,
Can Spring be far behind?

Truly, when we are struggling with what to do next, and with what will come next, faith that there is something planned for us is the only way to survive the stress of the unknown. When we wait and do not rush headlong into something, we know is not right we strengthen our patience. When we are confident that what we are waiting for will come, then all good things come to us.

This is when I reach for pen and my journal. Patience takes great courage, practice and the resolve that you cannot always determine the timeline for your life. There is a timeline, but not one that you can control completely. Again, you will see fear hidden behind the impatience. I often find courage by reflecting and, (surprise!) slowing down my thoughts. I am a doer by nature, so it is often difficult for me to sit and wait. You can imagine what fun I have trying to meditate. Let's take an impatient doer with a brain like a bag of cats and ask her to sit perfectly still in a quiet room and think about nothing. It's like asking the biggest chatty-Cathy you know to play the silence game. It amps up my spaz-quotient by a hundred. I still try to do it because when it works, it is very calming. I find that I reflect better with a pen in hand if I am sitting. If I need to be moving, I head for the outdoors. Going for a hike in a silent and beautiful place allows me to *wait actively*. Patience and waiting does not need to be a passive endeavor. Many times, the answer you are waiting for comes only when you are busy doing something else.

Allow me to share a personal joy-of waiting story. There was a point in 2007 when my life spun completely out of my control and no matter how much I tried to control it back into what I had carefully designed it to be, it just simply refused to cooperate. Between 2007 and 2011 I went through a divorce, two job losses and a disruptive illness. Yet through it all, I desperately wanted my relationship with Will to progress. And through it all I just kept hearing the Spirit tell me to be patient. At first this was a beast of a task. He had to want to marry me, right? Why wouldn't he want to drop everything and start an exciting life with me? Oh, except for three daughters, a large home, his own work and health issues and minor crisis of faith. Just those things. I prayed and prayed. I tried to make something happen, to force his hand. Finally, I understood that I needed to stop trying to change him and look at myself. I needed to understand that he was in love with me and he did want a future with me, but he also needed time. And so, did I. My impatience assumed that I was ready to be married again. My impatience assumed that *he* was the problem. *He* or *she* is never the problem, folks. It is always with us. Sometimes we wait and are finally told that it is time for us to move on. I was told to stop feeling like I always have to make a stand, that I always have to be the one who demands change from others. I finally understood that I needed to appreciate the man he is and accept what I knew deeply in my heart– that he and I are meant to be together and we have all of eternity to get it sorted out. That one thought – which was revealed while I was journaling – has brought my impatience and anxiety level down about 85%. There are still times when I get all wound up and try to push things with him, but then I remember that I know what I am waiting for and it is worth it, and it will come. Slowly, but surely, he is moving towards our future. With each small step, I thank my God that I was patient and did not leap out of the relationship out of pride and impatience and a mistaken belief that I deserved what I wanted in the exact moment I wanted it. If I had followed my impatience, then I would have missed out on so much joy that has happened since.

Life is not something that can be crafted, manipulated and set on a rigid timeline. Like love, it doesn't work that way. Not with our partners, our families, our children, our friends or our careers. Strong and meaningful relationships take time and patience. Instead of running headlong for something else or someone else, I made the decision to love Will, myself, and my life through patience. I learned the most important lesson of my life. When I run now, I run <u>towards</u> things and not <u>from</u> things. I am trying now to apply this to my career, which is an area where I still struggle with trying to control every move. I am trying to make decisions with a target in mind rather than with an escape in mind. Escape-based choices only solve half of the problem. Waiting for the right opportunity and the right time saves you from jumping from the proverbial frying pan in to the fire. This requires patience because it is difficult to stay in a tough situation while waiting for the right target to appear. Again, the only way to make progress is to practice patience with mental mantras and consciously slowing down and deciding to wait.

There is a fine line we must discuss. That is the line between patience and procrastination. Are you waiting or stalling? That is the question. What is your answer? Liane Cordes, in her book *The Reflecting Pond*, does a supreme reflection on the difference. She asserts that,

> "Patience is calm and rational. It is the result of confidence and hard work. I'm not 'putting off' anything because I've already done everything in my power to achieve my goal. Instead, I'm putting the results of my efforts in God's hands with the assurance I've done my best and can do no more."

The following activity is an adaptation

of her reflection.

Activity 1.19.2 The Procrastination Question

Cordes: "'The best way I know to tell the difference between patience and procrastination,' a friend said, 'is to look at my motives for my actions or inactions. If I delay doing something out of fear and self-doubt, then I'm procrastinating. I'm letting irrational emotions dictate my behavior. If, on the other hand, I delay doing something because I'm waiting for the outcome of something I've already worked on, that's patience.'"

1. Consider this reflection with the lens of a current life-situation that is testing your patience. What life situation are you considering? _____

2. Describe your behavior in terms of Cordes' words. Are you not acting because of fear or self-doubt? Or are you not acting because you are waiting for the results of work

you   have   done   previously?
_____ For instance, if you
have applied for ten jobs and are waiting for the
results of those applications, then you are using
patience while waiting. If you have applied for
a job, did not hear back and are not applying for
others out of a fear of rejection, then you are
procrastinating.

*3. Ask yourself and be honest with the
answer. "TODAY am I being patient or am I
procrastinating?"*

*4. Use this daily reflection to motivate
yourself: "I will not let fear or self-doubt govern
my behavior. I will stop procrastinating on the
things I need to do, and then I will patiently
place the results of my efforts in*

God's hands." Feel free to substitute
your belief in place of God so that the statement
is true to you.

After pages of text on the importance
of patience and waiting for good things to

come, perhaps the most important thing to remember is that self-improvement also takes patience, courage and kindness. You will not master patience today. I'm sorry, but you won't. It is, like everything, something that requires time and attention. If you allow yourself that time, you will find yourself in a place where you can calm your frustrations and accept your life more easily. You will treat others and yourself with greater kindness and you will uncover even greater things than what you thought you could create for yourself.

Demi-Chapter XX: Value You

To love yourself is to value yourself.
We do not often value ourselves enough. We have been taught that as "good people," regardless of our religion, we should embrace self-denial, self-sacrifice and humility. If we don't then we risk being labeled self-centered and egotistical. As a result, we have grown to look to others for happiness and blame outside forces when we miss it. Newman and Berkowitz, authors of *How to Be Your Own Best*

Friend, coined a phrase I feel targets what we fall victim to – they call it "negative self-hypnosis." This means that we label ourselves with negative titles to convince ourselves that we are not good enough, not worthy of being valued and, therefore, not arrogant or egotistical. Ironically, this false humility is exactly egotistical. It is a means of being completely self-focused (on our faults). Rather than honoring the blessings and talents that we have, we try to convince ourselves and others that because we are not perfect, we are not valuable. Instead of drawing attention to ourselves through kindness, charity, humility or excellence, we seek positive feedback by using false humility in hopes of garnering compliments.

For any of us who follow human models of spiritual teachings, we can learn that all of them, Jesus, Buddha, Mohammed, the Dali Lama, et cetera, all had self-acceptance as a crucial part of their lives. If they had not they would not have been able to turn their lives entirely outward to those around them in need. These men all accepted themselves and us as we are. Walter Trobisch wrote a book entitled *Love Yourself & Love Is a Feeling to Be Learned* in 1971. In it he writes that this unconditional love of ourselves makes it possible for us to accept ourselves and others. Not seeing everything you have inside of you and everything you do every day, only leads to a waste of your gifts, your blessings and your life.

Valuing yourself also means expecting that others value you. I have a desperate need to be needed. I have not yet uncovered the source of this need, but I do recognize it. I feel great compassion for others, and I feel it is my responsibility to use the blessings I have been given to improve the lives of those I encounter on earth. That said, I also dig feeling like I am valuable in the lives of others. At work this means that what I do has meaning. At home, it means that what I do makes life a little nicer for people I care for. The dark side of this is that I feel a little sad when I am not needed to make dinner or when what I do goes unappreciated. This is not to say that I am not valued by others. This is an example of how I am still not entirely valuing myself and my contribution to this world? I have worked long and hard on valuing myself and finding ways to feel my own worth. I am still working.

"No one needs to continue life with a wounded soul (Trobisch)." You deserve to be loved and you deserve to love yourself. It is not a failing to see your own worth. This has been a long road for me, and you can see that I am not at the finish line, but I have more positive thoughts about myself now than negative ones.   I would never have even considered writing a book like this five years ago because I truly felt I had nothing to write that anyone wanted to read. I understand now that writing is a gift for me and it is my responsibility to use it to the benefit of others.

I had to heal my soul and find my voice first.

Activity 1.20.1 Read & Reflect 2

Read the statement from Jennifer Hatmaker below. In the space provided, in your journal, or in your head, make a note of your first response to the statement. Then dig deep and privately record how it makes you feel. We aren't trying to solve any problems here. Just feel and write. Cry, get angry, write until your hand hurts – this may bring out a lot of emotion – let it.

> *"You are worthy of basic human respect just because you are alive. No one should demean, mock, or humiliate you. You should not stand for that behavior. That is not the way of Christ, neither on the giving or receiving end."*

Being proud of yourself is okay. Recognize your own worth yet maintain humility. Know in your heart that you are not the end-all and the be-all of the universe, but you are worthy of love and respect and you deserve to be valued.

How can you learn to value yourself? Clearly, I am not saying that I am an expert at this. I am learning too. First and foremost, we need to learn to listen to ourselves. Here is a positive reason to say that you hear voices. We tend to learn to ignore ourselves – the cheering section in our heads. We hear only the naysayers and the critics. We drown out the good things, like we forget to hear the birds singing when we are walking on a crowded street. They are still singing; we just blend them in with everything else. Your internal birds are also singing, if you stop to listen. Learning to hear them again takes practice and consciously quieting the negativity. You can borrow my Dwayne Johnson henchman if you want, but I'll need him back.

Iyanla Vanzant, author, life coach, and Oprah magazine contributor encourages you to not only value who you are, what you have accomplished and what you want; she prompts you to ask for it. Part of valuing yourself is having the courage and belief in yourself to ask for what you want. She adds that if you don't believe in yourself enough to be open to receiving what you want, then you will not get it. I deeply admire Will's eldest daughter for her ability to ask for what she wants in life. I am often too shy or afraid to ask – thinking that I am putting other people out or I should be strong enough to get it myself. She believes she is worthy and deserving of every good and beautiful thing. Even when she doesn't get all she wants; she gets more than she had. It fascinates me. At some point, everyone fears that they will fall short. She is the manifestation of Norman Vincent Peale's advice to "Shoot for the moon. Even if you miss, you'll still land amongst the stars."

Newman and Berkowitz tell us in their book, *How to Be Your Own Best Friend*, that it is our responsibility to recognize our own value. Believe that you are good enough and that your life brings an irreplaceable value to this life – and everyone in it. When we wait for others to recognize our worth, we end up resentful or sad. Often when it does come, we feel conflicted and dismiss it only as flattery. The only compliments that truly stick are often the ones we give ourselves. When we see and acknowledge our skills, talents, blessings and contributions, we are adding value to our own accounting sheet of worth. I do not always give myself the compliments that I should, but I am learning how to recognize all I bring to the lives of those around me.

Activity 1.20.3 Your List of Assets

In this activity, I am going to ask you to think about all that you bring to the world. I know that this can be tough sometimes, but I am going to ask you to intentionally toot your asset horn.

1)   *Pick a day you would like to focus on. It*

could be today, or yesterday or last Saturday. Write that day: _____

2)   *Without stopping, hesitating, judging, evaluating or editing, list all of the things you did that day that you can remember. You may need to consult a calendar to refresh your memory.*

3)   *Now, look at the list and circle all of the things you did that positively impacted this world in some way. As you circle, think about how you positively impacted the world. I want you to be honest and I want you to be positive. You may feel that you are being a little liberal with your praise, but YOU SHOULD BE!* For example, if I think about today, I would circle that I made breakfast for Will and this made him feel loved and cared for. I positively impacted his life. Then I swept the floor, which is impactful for calmness in our household. Then I wrote twenty pages, which is impactful, I hope, for my readers.

4)   If valuing yourself is an area of growth for you, I would encourage you to use this

activity as a nightly journal activity. You don't need to always write and circle. Once you get better at it you may be able to do it entirely in your heart.

5) If you are really struggling with this activity, find a trusted friend, family member, lover or colleague and ask them to get you started by telling you how you have positively impacted the world. You may be surprised by all you have done and all they have credited you with.

Saturday Night Live's character Will Smalley made jest of the personal affirmation: "I'm good enough. I'm smart enough. And, darn it! People like me." I was a teenager when that hit the airwaves and I thought it was ridiculous. Being a wiser person now, I rather value the idea of daily affirmation. While that one, specifically, makes me laugh, it is also one that I like to repeat to myself. Probably because it makes me laugh and, darn it, I like laughing.

Activity 1.20.4 Personal Affirmation

Our last activity for this book is for you to write or find your own personal affirmation. This affirmation will meet your needs right now. It will help you value yourself and remember that you are worthy of respect and love. You may find you need to change your affirmation as life changes. When that happens, just come back and write a new one. If you need ideas or more guidance, see Julia Cameron's *The Artist's Way*.

1. Do you have a personal affirmation that reminds you of your self-worth and personal value to the world? If yes, write it here and say it to yourself every time you doubt that you are awesome. _____

2. If you do not yet have a personal affirmation, you can start to write one here. This activity is like Mad Libs for the Tortured Soul (Maybe the title my next book!). Another option is to start to look for one in the world around you – check out the Amish gift shops.

Use these sentence starters to get you thinking.

- *I am _____ enough for _____.*
- *I accept my _____.*
- *I do not need others to tell me how _____ I am.*
- *I believe for myself that I am _____.*
- *My _____ gives me value in this world.*
- *Today I changed _____'s life for the better.*
- *I am _____ and I deserve _____.*
- *I may look _____ but I am tough as _____.*
- *Today I feel really great about myself because I _____.*
- *Today I salute myself for being able to rise above _____.*

3. Write your own. What makes you realize how incredibly special and valuable you are? What will remind you to never devalue yourself again?

I turn to the artist P!NK (and her cowriters Alecia Moore, Max Martin, and Johan Schuster) for our final reminder of how vital it is to always value ourselves with a portion of her song "F***in' Perfect." Feel free to sing along, but remember that you can love yourself without being perfect.

> *You're so mean (you're so*
> *mean) when you talk (when you*
> *talk) about yourself*
> *you were wrong*
> *Change those voices (change*
> *those voices) in your head (in*
> *your head)*
> *Make them like you instead*
> *So complicated look how big*
> *you'll make it*
> *filled with so much hatred*
> *Such a tired game*
> *It's enough I've done all I can*
> *think of*
> *chased down all my demons*
> *I've seen you do the same*
> *Pretty, pretty please*
> *Don't you ever, ever feel*
> *Like you're less than Less than*
> *perfect*

Pretty, pretty, please
If you ever, ever feel
Like you're nothing
You are perfect to me

May you be perfect enough for yourself, my friends. Only you can recognize your true value to this life.

Epilogue

You have reached the end of the first book in this series of three. It appears that you have not gone blind after all these pages of self-love. Now you can say "I told you so" to anyone who assails you with accusations about the recklessness of learning to love yourself for who you are. I hope that you have found it thought-provoking, entertaining and valuable. If you liked this one, stay tuned for *Book Two: The Golden Rule Is for Sissies & Other Lies They Told You About Loving Others* and *Book Three: Life Sucks, Then You Die & Other Lies They Told You About Loving Your Life*

My friends and readers, I have learned so much about myself and love while writing this book. I have done the exercises along with you and I am discovering every day how to love myself better so that I can love others as they deserve to be loved. It would awesome and fulfilling if everyone loved me and you, but they won't, and even if they did it can't compare to the satisfaction of loving yourself. May you continue forward on your journey with love for yourself, knowing that you are loved and needed by all of us. And I promise, you won't go blind for doing it.

Referenced Works, Resources, Recommended and Otherwise Really Good Readings

Referenced Works/ Resources – Used by expressed permission.

A.Byley. Your ecard. Encouragement. "While I was running today I heard someone clapping, it was just my thighs cheering me on." https://www.someecards.com/usercards/viewcard/MjAxMi03MmE1ZDZkZmU1N2Y3ZmUy/?tagSlug=encouragement

"A booby doing its mating dance." Wolfgang Kaehler/LightRocket, via Getty Images. https://www.nytimes.com/2017/03/06/science/galapagos-blue-footedboobies.html

Anderson, Joan. *A Weekend to Change Your Life: Find Your Authentic Self after a Lifetime of Being All Things to All People*. Used by permission of Broadway Books, an imprint of the Crown Publishing Group, a division of Penguin Random House, LLC. All rights reserved. New York: 2006. Print.

Bach, Richard. Quote. Downloaded May 15, 2015https://www.google.com/search?sit

e =&source=hp&q=richard+bach&oq
=richard&gs_l=psyab.1.0.35i39k1j0
i67k1l2j0i20k1.5745.7873.0.10684.8.7.
0.0.0.0.285.1096.1j5j1.7.0....0...
1.1.64.psyab..1.7.1096.0..0i131k1.4KlL
J1oDu-k&safe=active&ssui=on

Beck, Martha. The Oprah Magazine. Print.

- "To Change or Not to Change?"
  September 2014:48, "Escape Your Rat
  Race" February 2014:39-40,
- "Don't Blow It" March 2014:41,
- "Holiday Time … And the Giving Is
  Easy" December 2014:48,
- "It's All About What You Do with
  Your Breakthrough" August 2014: 94-
  95,
- "Don't Ask" February 2015:36,
- "Your Intuition Has Something to Tell
  You" May 2015:149-153,
- "The Role of a Lifetime" June 2015:35.

Brooks, Garth & Blazy, Kent. "How You Ever
  Gonna Know." Lyrics. *Sevens*. 1997.

Boyack, Merrilee. *Toss the Guilt and Catch the
  Joy*. Salt Lake City: ©Deseret Book
  Company, 2008. Print. p.89. Used by
  permission.

Burroughs, Augusten. *Magical Thinking: True
  Stories*. New York: St. Martin's, 2004.
  Print. Downloaded from
  https://www.goodreads.com/author/
  quotes/3058.Augusten_Burroughs on
  August 10, 2015.

Coelho, Paulo. *The Alchemist*. New York: Harper, 1988. Print. pp. vi, viii, 22, 62, 130.

Cordes, Liana. *The Reflecting Pond. Meditations for Self-Discovery*. New York: HarperCollins, 1981 Print. p.92. Reprinted by permission.

Covey, Stephen. *The 7 Habits of Highly Effective People.* New York: Simon & Schuster, Inc. 1989. Print. p.151.

F***in' Perfect Words and Music by Alecia Moore, Max Martin and Johan Schuster Copyright © 2010 EMI Blackwood Music Inc., Pink Inside Publishing and Maratone AB All Rights for EMI Blackwood Music Inc. and Pink Inside Publishing Administered by Sony/ATV Music Publishing LLC, 424 Church Street, Suite 1200, Nashville, TN 37219 All Rights for Maratone AB Administered by Kobalt Music Publishing America, Inc. International Copyright Secured All Rights Reserved Reprinted by Permission of Hal Leonard LLC.

Hate Yourself (Life's Too Short) Words and Music by Hillary Lindsey and Brett James Copyright © 2006 BMG Gold Songs, Stage Three Songs, Reservoir Media Music and Sony/ATV Music Publishing LLC All Rights for BMG Gold Songs Administered by BMG Rights Management (US) LLC All

Rights for Stage Three Songs
Administered by Stage Three Music
(US) Inc., a BMG Chrysalis company
All Rights for Sony/ATV Music
Publishing LLC Administered by
Sony/ATV Music Publishing LLC, 424
Church Street, Suite 1200, Nashville,
TN 37219 All Rights Reserved Used by
Permission Reprinted by Permission of
Hal Leonard LLC

Hatmaker, Jen. *For the Love: Fighting for
Grace in a World of Impossible
Standards*.Nashville: Nelson, 2015.
Print. pp. 20-21, 32, 34, 136, 203 Used
by permission of Thomas Nelson.
www.thomasnelson.com.

Henry, Todd. CASE Convention 2015,
Breckenridge, Colorado. "Unleashing
Your Passion, Focus and Brilliance at
Work." July 29, 2015.

Hochman, David. "A Wise and Witty Dame"
The AARP Magazine June/July
2014:25. Print. Reprinted from the
June-July issue of *AARP The Magazine*
article by David Hochman. Copyright
2014 AARP. All rights reserved.

McDonald, Shawn. "Lovely." Song lyrics.
Downloaded 7 July
2015.http://www.godtube.com/artist/sh
aw n-mcdonald/

Morrow Lindbergh, Anne. *Gift From The Sea.*
Used by permission of Pantheon Books,
an imprint of the Knopf Doubleday

Publishing Group, a division of Penguin Random House LLC. New York: 1955: 26.

Murphy, Brian. "Interactive Map: Life Expectancy by Texas County." *Texas Tribune*. April 25, 2012. Downloaded July 13, 2014. https://www.texastribune.org/library /data/updated-life-expectancytotals/

Newman, Mildred, Berkowitz, Bernard and Owen, Jean. *How to Be Your Own Best Friend.* Toronto: Random House, 1971. Print.

Niebuhr, Reinhold. "The Serenity Prayer." 1951.http://www.inkmonkey.com/seren it y-prayer.html

Oaks, Dallin H. "In His Own Time, In His Own Way" *Ensign* August 2013:24. Print.

Poindexter, Linda. "Be Proud of Mistakes." Board of Wisdom quote #42198. Downloaded 2.19.2015. https://boardofwisdom.com/togo/?vi ewid=1005&listname=General&star t=42191&viewid=1005&listname= General&start=42191#.Wa4aSch96 M9

Ponder, Stephanie. "Enjoy Life More by Doing Less." *The Costco Connection* June 2015: 32. Print.

Radmacher, Mary Anne. "Live with Intention." https://livelifehappy.com/?s=radma cher. Downloaded 9.4.2017.

Rasmus, Carolyn J. *Simplify: A Guide to*

Caring for the Soul. Salt Lake: Deseret Book. 2007. Print. p.112.

Renlund, Dale G. "Latter-Day Saints Keep On Trying." April 5, 2015:56. Print.

Robinson, Ken, and Lou Aronica. *The Element: How Finding Your Passion Changes Everything*. New York: Viking, 2009. Print.

Rowling, J.K. *Harry Potter and the Sorcerer's Stone*. New York: Scholastic, 1997. Print. p. 214.

Rubin, Gretchen. *The Happiness Project: Or Why I Spent a Year Trying to Sing in the Morning, Clean My Closets, Fight Right, Read Aristotle, and Generally Have More Fun*. New York, NY: Harper, 2009. Print. p. 19, 20, 21, 35, 66, 170, 250.

Sheen, Fulton. Downloaded 11.24.2017. https://www.goodreads.com/author/show/2412.Fulton_J_Sheen

Stanford, Dan. Think Exist. Downloaded. 10.8.2015 http://thinkexist.com/quotation/expe rience_is_what_you_get_when_you_do n-t_get/13116.html

Trobisch, Walter. *Love Yourself & Love Is a Feeling to Be Learned*. Boliver, Missouri: Quiet Waters Publishing. 2001.

"Unused Vacation Days: Why Workers Take a Pass." CNNMoney. Cable News Network, 18 May 2012. Downloaded.

06 August 2016.
http://money.cnn.com/2012/05/18/n
ews/economy/unused_vacation_day
s/index.htm

Wonder, Stevie. Quotation. Downloaded
9.10.2017.https://www.brainyquote.co
m/quotes/quotes/s/steviewond120630.ht
ml

*Recommended and Otherwise Really Good
Readings*

While these informed the author, they are not
directly cited in the text.

1 Corinthians 13:4-7. Downloaded. 30 July
2016.
https://www.biblegateway.com/passa
ge/?search=1+Corinthians+13%3A4-
8&version=CEB

"60-Second Health Boosters." *AARP Magazine*
June-July 2014: 14. Print.

"A Moment for You" *Woman's World.*
September 1, 2014: 40. Print.

"A Moment for You" *Woman's World.*
September 29, 2014: 42. Print.

Ardern, Ian S. "Shunning Temptation" *Ensign*
February 2014:56-59. Print.

Arnold-Ratliff, Katie. "Elizabeth Gilbert, In
Full Bloom." *The Oprah Magazine*
October 2013:182. Print.

Basnicki, Erica. "Interview: David Hendy,
author of *Noise: A Human History.*

September 5, 2013 accessed August 14, 2016.http://designingsound.org/2013/09/i nterview-david-hendy-author-ofnoise-a-human-history/

Bednar, David. "Therefore They Hushed Their Fears" *Ensign* April 4, 2015: 46. Print.

Bertsche, Rachel. "An Attitude of Gratitude" *The Oprah Magazine* November 2014:129. Print.

Biswas-Diener, Robert, PhD. *The Courage Quotient: How Science Can Make You Braver.* John Wiley & Sons printed by Jossey-Bass. 2012.

Brown, Brené. *The Oprah Magazine.* Print.
- "Dare to Reality Check Your Expectations" June 2014:48, "Dare to Recharge. October 2014:58,
- "Dare to Get Real" August 2014:54.

Campbell Exner, Judith. Quotation. Downloaded. 9.10.2017. http://www.azquotes.com/quote/584670

Clayton, L. Whitney. "Choose to Believe." *Ensign* April 4, 2015:36. Print.

Cohen, Arianne. "The Smartest Marriage Advice We've Ever Heard" *Ladies' Home Journal* May 2014: 54. Print.

"Conversation Feeds the Soul." *The Oprah Magazine. Print.* Ellen DeGeneres December 2009:128, Selma Hayek September 2003:2 http://www.oprah.com/omagazine/Oprah-Interviews- Actress-andProducer-Salma-Hayek.

Duvall, Robert. "What I Know Now." *AARP The Magazine* June/July 2014:13. Print.

Dyer, Wayne. *10 Secrets for Success and Inner Peace*. Carlsbad, CA: Hay House, Inc. 2001. Print.

Englewood Church of Christ. "24 Ways to Have a Better Life." *Weekly Bulletin* April 2008.

Girdwain, Jessica. "Healthy You: 7 Ways to Lose Those Last 5 Pounds" *AARP The Magazine* June/July 2014:17. Print.

Grant, Meg. "Finding a Light in the Darkness" *AARP The Magazine* April/May 2014:48. Print.

Graziano Breuning, Loretta, PhD. "Life Lessons" *Real Simple* April 2014:68. Print.

"Greatest Pep Talk Ever" *The Oprah Magazine.* January 2015:91. Print.

Fliess, Sue. "Ordinary Moments That Will Change the Way You View the World (and Yourself)." O Magazine Online. Downloaded 8.14.2014: http://www.oprah.com/spirit/howto-make-every-moment-matter-suefliess#ixzz4rlqQUcvK"

Funnell, Martha. "Blood Glucose and Your Brain." *Diabetes and You* Fall 2014:8. Print.

Halbreich, Betty. Secrets of a Fashion Therapist. Downloaded from Q The Stylist. June 27, 2015 http://www.qthestylist.com/about

Harper, Jennifer. "84 percent of the world
     population has faith; a third are
     Christian." *The Washington Times -
     December 23, 2012, 11:05AM*
     Accessed 8.21.2016.
     http://www.washingtontimes.com/bl
     og/watercooler/2012/dec/23/84percent-
     world-population-has-faiththird-are-ch/.
Jacobson, Malia. "Help others, help yourself."
     The Costco Connection June 2015:45.
     Print.
Jalal Al Din Rumi
     .https://www.poets.org/poetsorg/poet/ja
     lal-al-din-rumi
Jones, Edward. "Breathe" *Real Simple* March
     2015:54. Print.
Kearns, Brenda. "Lower Your Cancer Risk
     with Healthy Gums" *Woman's World*
     October 6, 2014: 15.
Kohan, Jenji, "Words I Live By." *The Oprah
     Magazine* June 2014: 24. Print.
Kunz, Elizabeth. "Life Lessons" *Real Simple*
     October 2014:62. Print.
Leavitt, Mindy Anne. "Life More Abundant"
     Ensign December 2014:12-15. Print.
Levine. Beth. "Is Stress Contagious?" *The
     Oprah Magazine* June 2014:82. Print.
Lewis, Sarah, PhD. "The Rise: Creativity, The
     Gift of Failure, and Search for
     Mastery." Conference talk. Colorado
     Association of School Executives, July
     30, 2015.
McGraw, Phil C., Ph.D. *The Oprah Magazine.*

Print:

- "The Way You Do Anything Is the Way You Do Everything." September 2014:54.
- "Never Miss a Good Chance to Shut Up." March 2014:48.
- "How Much Fun Are You To Live With?" December 2014:54.
- "Winners Do Things Losers Don't Want To Do" August 2014:50. "You've Got to Pick a Horse and Ride It." June 2014:46.
- "Look Where You're Going, Not Where You've Been." October 2014:56.
- "There Is Power in Forgiveness" January 2015:41.
- "How to Get Over Rejection" March 2015: 39.

Miller, Mark. "Surviving the Jolt" *AARP The Magazine* May 2014:56. Print.

Monroe, Valerie. "Seeing Yourself with New Eyes." Life Lessons. The Oprah Magazine. September 2014.

Murphy, Tim. "Made for More Than Walking" *The New York Times Style Magazine September 12, 2014:*232. Print.

Neville, Beverly Hyatt. "Nourishing Our Bodies and Our Spirits." *Ensign* February 2014: 71.

Nolan, Michael. Goodreads. Downloaded 8 August 2017.

https://www.goodreads.com/author/
quotes/136408.Michael_Nolan .

Ogletree, Mark. "Speak, Listen, & Love"
Ensign February 2014:14-17. Print.

Oz, Mehmet, M.D. The Oprah Magazine. Print.
- "The New Risk Factor," February
2014:46.
- "Dr. Oz's Health Challenge" June
2015:43.
- "Dr. Oz's 5 Health Tips That Will
- Never Get Old" June 2014.

Pearson, Kevin W. "Stay by the Tree" Ensign
April 5, 2015:114. Print.

Ratledge, Ingela. "Wait For It." Real Simple
May 2014:111-112. Print.

Robbins, Alexander. "The Power of Quirk:
Why What Sets You Apart Actually
Helps You Succeed." Real Simple Oct.
2014: 138. Print.

Schulman, Helen. "Where you go, I will
follow." Real Simple. February 2014:
41. Print.

Scott, Richard G. "Living A Life of Peace, Joy,
and Purpose." Commencement Speech
at Brigham Young University. Ensign
April 12, 2011:37-41.

Spencer, Octavia. "My Best Life" The Oprah
Magazine March 2015:21. Print.

Svoboda, Elizabeth. "The Morality Workout"
The Oprah Magazine:79. Print.

Stevenson, Gary E. "The Reality of
Christmas" Ensign December 2014:25.
Print.

"The Joys of Letting Go" Kaiser Permanente
 Newsletter
Sunny Sea Gold. "Life Lessons" *Real Simple*.
 October 2014:68. Print.
The Secrets of Joy. A Treasury of Wisdom.
 Philadelphia: Running Press. 1995.
Uchtdorf, Dieter F. "Grateful in Any
 Circumstances" *Ensign* May 2014:75.
 Print.
Vanzant, Iyanla. "Iyanla, Fix My Life!" *The*
 Oprah Magazine. Print.
 • "How Do I Conquer Indecision?"
  September 2014:56.
 • "How Do I Ask for What I Want?"
  December 2014:56.
 • "How Do I Know When It's Time to
  Let Go?" May 2014:48.
 • "How Do I Stay Hopeful About the
  Future?" March 2014:54.
Vasa, Monisha, PhD. "Develop a child's
 awareness." *The Costco Connection*
 June 2015:43. Print.
Whitney, Clayton, L. "Choose to Believe"
 Ensign April 4, 2015:36. Print.
Wildgen, Michelle. "Moments of Grace" *The*
 Oprah Magazine December 2014:141.
 Print.
Winfrey, Oprah. "What I Know for Sure" *The*
 Oprah Magazine. Print.
 • June 2015:120,
 • October 2014:172,
 • June 2014:160,

- May 2014:150,
- March 2014:146,
- November 2014:168,
- March 2015:124.

Wubbels, Lance. *I Wish For You. Gentle Reminders to Follow Your Heart.* Minneapolis: Koechel Peterson and Associates, Published 2009 by Gift Books from Hallmark, 2009. Print. p.78.

Made in the USA
Coppell, TX
19 May 2021

55984929R00192